LIBERIA

Will
Rise
Again

Arthur F. Kulah

LIBERIA

Will Rise Again

REFLECTIONS ON THE LIBERIAN CIVIL CRISIS

ABINGDON PRESS
Nashville

LIBERIA WILL RISE AGAIN
Reflections on the Liberian Civil Crisis

Copyright © 1999 by Abingdon Press

Scripture quotations in this publication, unless otherwise indicated, are from the New Revised Standard Version of the Bible, copyrighted © 1989 by the Division of Christian Education of the National Council of the Churches of Christ in the United States of America, and are used by permission. All rights reserved.

Library of Congress Cataloging-in-Publication Data
Kulah, Arthur F., 1936-
    Liberia will rise again : reflections on the Liberian civil crisis / Arthur F. Kulah.
        p.   cm.
    ISBN 0-687-07594-7 (alk. paper)
    1. Liberia—History—Civil War, 1989-   I. Title.
DT636.5.K85   1999
966.6203—dc21   98-50431
                                                                                CIP

This book is printed on acid–free paper.

99 00 01 02 03 04 05 06 07 08-10 9 8 7 6 5 4 3 2 1

This book is dedicated to
three important women in my life:

❊ Mrs. Francis Taylor Echols
my American mother of South Dallas, Texas,
who with her late husband, Dr. T. B. Echols,
adopted and educated me from
elementary school through college.

❊ *My late mother,* Yau Zonpu Kulah,
who tasted death at my birth
to give me life.

❊ *My dear wife,* Violet Mamusu,
who stands by, supports, and mothers me
along the way.

———————————

This book is also dedicated to
the children of Liberia,
particularly my grandchildren.

CONTENTS

ACKNOWLEDGMENTS

LOST to memory are the names of countless individuals and their contributions to the writing and publication of this book. Even so, a few of them readily come to mind. Among them are the Rev. Levi C. Williams II, who transcribed a few chapters that were recorded and who typed and edited several chapters; Mr. John R. Kollie; Mrs. Ora Kollies, my secretary; Bartum and Clarise Kulah; J. Lamark and Dixine Cox; Herbert and Mary Zigbuo, Mai Roberts-Cooper; Alfred A. Kulah; Counselor Lawrence A. Morgan; Elijah S. Ghanty; Yei R. Wuor; and Richard Clarke.

My indebtedness also goes to others in and out of Liberia with whom I had discussions and interviews that led and inspired and encouraged me to write this book.

May God bless them all.

WHY do people fight wars? The motives that have usually been the basis for open armed conflict include the struggle for land, for wealth, for power, or for the sake of honor. No matter what justifiable reasons a people or group may have for declaring and waging war against another group of people, the effects are disastrous and destructive, tearing down in hours what took years to build.

For almost a decade, Liberia, Africa's oldest republic, was involved in a war of such great magnitude that it cost the lives of more than 200,000 people and millions, if not billions, of dollars in destruction of property and infrastructure. For seven years, while the war in Liberia raged, peace conferences were held, treaties and accords signed, only to be broken by one or another of the parties to the conflict.

The Economic Community of West African States (ECOWAS) initiated efforts as far back as 1990 to end the conflict; but for seven years, Liberia seemed to be held in the claws of a helpless, hopeless situation, going in a vicious cycle of violence, death, and destruction. The agreement in 1996 by the so-called "warring factions," which numbered five in all, to finally abide by the Abuja Accord—thus ceasing hostilities against one another and against the people of Liberia—brought sighs of cautious relief.

On January 31, 1997, after a tedious journey toward order and stability, and in consonance with the Abuja Accord, the warring factions ceased to exist. This was the result of a negotiated settlement reached by the factions through the efforts of ECOWAS, the Organization of African Unity (OAU), the United Nations (UN), and well-meaning Liberian groups such as the InterFaith Mediation Committee (IFMC, made up of leaders representing religious groups in the country). Not only did the factions agree to dissolve their various military organizations, they also consented to disarm and demobilize their soldiers and participate in presidential and general elections.

Up to the point of this writing, the disarmament process has produced laudable results and peace is now at hand. The vigilance of ECOMOG (the military arm of ECOWAS) in the search for arms and ammunition after the official voluntary disarmament date resulted in the discovery of large caches of weapons and ammunition in various areas formerly under the control of dissolved warring factions. The most notable discovery was an armory in the home of former ULIMO-K leader Alhaji Kromah on March 7, 1997, two months after the official deadline of voluntary disarmament. After a public apology and an explanation that the arms were intended to be turned over to ECOMOG, the charges against Mr. Kromah were dropped. The political debate leading to elections was active because the stability of Liberia is the primary concern of every Liberian.

The war is over, but there are lessons to be learned so that this ugly phenomenon does not recur. This "Glorious Land of Liberty" is emerging from the abyss of war and destruction to take its place among the civilized nations of the world. As Liberians, with the help of the international community, forge a nation out of the remnants of devastation and madness, we need to keep focused and to move toward a future where all Liberians, regardless of tribe, religion, or class, will feel a sense of belonging and oneness.

This book attempts to outline the causes and events of the war, to provide some interpretation of the situation, and to point out suggestions that can be followed to a brighter future for Liberia. Before getting into the core of the discussion, however, it seems necessary to spend some time exploring the nature of the war in Liberia. This will help the reader understand the magnitude of the darkest seven years in Liberia's history.

From June 24 to 27, 1984, the second of two conferences on terrorism was sponsored by the Jonathan Institute, a private foundation devoted to research on terrorism and related issues. As a result of that conference, *Terrorism: How the West Can Win* (Farrar, Straus, Giroux; 1986), a book edited by Benjamin Netanyahu, Israeli Prime Minister, was published. One of the enlightening articles in the book is "The Totalitarian Confusion," by Jeane Kirkpatrick, former United States Ambassador to the United Nations.

In that article, Kirkpatrick makes distinctions between terrorism and conventional war as well as between terrorism and a war of liberation. Both terrorism and conventional wars, she observes, have political motives, except that a conventional war is fought against "armed enemies" and violence is used "where a state of belligerence is recognized to exist" (Netanyahu: 56–57).

Conventional war is usually waged by a state for legitimate reasons such as the defense of its citizens, defense of its territorial integrity, or protection of its sovereignty. A conventional war may be fought across the border with another country; or, if a nation harbors the enemies of another nation, the nation feeling threatened could pursue its enemies within that country and may be protected by international charters. For example, when Israeli troops stormed Entebbe Airport in Uganda, in East Africa, on July 4, 1976, this was a legitimate use of force because the "country of Uganda and its armed forces assisted and protected the terrorists" who had hijacked and endangered citizens of another state, Israel (Netanyahu: 183). Israel's response corresponded with conventional warfare since Israel was defending its citizens.

Was the war in Liberia a conventional war? Was the National Patriotic Front of Liberia (NPFL) defending and protecting Liberia's territory or its sovereignty? In the first place, the war was not declared by the government of Liberia but was declared against the government of Liberia. If the government in power at the time had attacked the NPFL and chased them into Ivory Coast, it would have been justified since the Armed Forces of Liberia (AFL) would have been defending Liberian territory and its citizens.

At the start of the war, the fighters described themselves as "freedom fighters," implying that this was a war of liberation. If "freedom fighters" are those who fight against imperialism and colonialism or even seek secession, could the warring factions be described as "liberators"? Few persons will agree they were "liberators."

In her essay, Kirkpatrick recognized a close relationship between terrorism and totalitarianism in that "both attempt to confuse as well as to terrorize. . . . Violence is used to maintain a system of lies, and lies are used to justify relations based on violence" (Netanyahu: 59).

With reference to Liberia, one can aptly describe the civil war as a war of terrorism in which the warring factions attempted to establish a system of totalitarianism in which they had complete control. If "terrorism is the deliberate and systematic murder, maiming, and menacing of the innocent to inspire fear for political ends" (Netanyahu: 9), then ultimately, the warring factions that existed in Liberia were terrorist organizations. Even though some of the warring factions argued that they came into existence to pressure the NPFL and to defend the land and people, they all adopted terrorist methods. Under their leadership, they sought to establish Liberia as a totalitarian state where only a few persons made the laws to suit themselves. They ruled the country in the interest of those who fought to come to power; and left to themselves, they would remain in power by force.

The war in Liberia was a war of shifting agendas; goals and objectives were changed at will to fit the purpose of the perpetrators. First the warring factions claimed the war was to overthrow the Doe government. When the Doe regime collapsed, and the war continued, it became clear that the warring factions were fighting to gain economic and political power and not for the benefit of the Liberian people. The parties to the conflict existed for themselves. During the seven years of catastrophe, the leaders of these organizations and their henchmen exploited the resources of the land and made illegal sale of these resources without benefit to the government and the people; they destroyed the social and moral fabric of the nation and made Liberia a useless, ungovernable, forsaken, and deserted country.

Even if the warring factions argue that they were not terrorist organizations, was their struggle just? Both Saint Augustine of Hippo (A.D. 354–430) and Saint Thomas Aquinas (A.D. 1225–1274) agreed, a war can only be declared by the state; second, the purpose ought to be the establishment of a just and better social order; third, war is to defend women and children and to protect lives; and fourth, a just war restricts itself to military targets.

At the start of the war, NPFL followers claimed they were fighting to usher in improved standards of living. Their intentions may have been just, but what they did proved to be the opposite. No new, just, and better socioeconomic order was established; the main victims were women and children; and the targets of attack had no limit because schools, churches, hospitals, embassies, and United Nations buildings were not spared. Was the war in Liberia just?

We cannot turn back the hands of time, but Liberians must covenant among themselves never to fight each other as we did from 1990 to 1997; diversity and difference must be a normal part of our existence.

This book does not seek to open old wounds but to openly discuss the issues, facilitate healing, and outline the problems we can learn from. The optimistic title, LIBERIA WILL RISE AGAIN, reflects the author's vision for Liberia's future. The first chapter, "How We Got There," traces the origins and possible causes of the war. Also included in the chapter is the reaction of the government of Liberia under President Samuel Kanyan Doe and the various attempts by the people of Liberia, the Economic Community of West African States (ECOWAS), the Inter-Faith Mediation Committee (IFMC), and the larger international community to achieve peace through constructive means.

Chapter 2, "From Sorrow to Joy," discusses the coming of the Liberian National Transitional Government and the arrival of the former warring faction leaders into Monrovia. The hopes aroused by the coming of these leaders and the problems emanating therefrom are presented.

As the war in Liberia raged on, certain persons and groups were benefiting and becoming rich. The third chapter, "Who Benefits," explores this problem. The idea that Liberia was being plundered while innocent persons were dying is examined. All of this was done in the name of "revolution," and the problem of revolutions advocating one thing and practicing another is the subject matter of Chapter 4, "What's the Difference?" The revolution of 1980 under the People's Redemption Council (PRC) and the revolution of 1990 led by Charles Taylor of the NPFL are examined. The chapter closes with some thoughts on the leadership of the Liberian National Transitional Government.

The war itself was started due to internal and external factors. Chapter 5 looks at the internal causes or ways in which Liberians themselves may have contributed to the problem. "The Problem Within" focuses on the public policies, the institutions, and the systems of nation building, particularly during the Tubman regime from 1944 to 1971, that should have provided good governance but were not properly developed, thus undermining the stability and order of the nation.

While there were internal problems, Chapter 6 points out the external factors that stimulated the crisis long before 1980. "Better Late Than Never" contends that the United States of America ought to play a more significant role in the development of Liberia, which it was instrumental in founding.

One of the consequences of the war is the internal displacement or the refugee situation it created. Liberians are not normally a traveling people, but scores of Liberians had to seek refuge in neighboring African countries and beyond. "Neighbors Indeed," Chapter 7, looks at how Liberians fared and were treated as refugees, especially in Ivory Coast, Ghana, and Guinea. Chapter 8, "Thank God For ECOMOG," recognizes the role the military arm of ECOWAS played in bringing the Liberian war to an end and in helping maintain stability and order.

The book closes in Chapter 9, "Liberia Will Rise Again," with some projection on how Liberians can make their country better than it was through hard work, integrity, self-respect, discipline, and determination.

Although the larger community is being called upon to assist Liberia to rise from degradation, Liberians themselves still have the greater responsibility of developing their country and moving it forward.

ONE

HOW WE GOT THERE

NOT many persons were really surprised that a war broke out in Liberia. As far back as 1980 or even 1947, some knew that one day Liberia would become engulfed in a civil war. However, what surprised most people was the intensity and cruelty shown by Liberians in the war. Considered peaceful and hospitable, the Liberians' sadistic bahavior shocked many in the world. It was equally surprising to realize that the ethnic divisions were as deep as have been revealed.

The decade of the 1980's was a stormy era. Beginning with the coup d'etat on April 12, 1980, the military government under the leadership of head of state and later president, Samuel Kanyan Doe, ruled with such iron handedness that in some circles the government was described as ranking with or worse than that of dictator Idi Amin who ruled Uganda in the 1970's.

While the military was in the forefront as leaders of the coup, a wider circle of politicians and professionals was opposed to the regime of President William R. Tolbert and the political domination of Liberia by the Americo-Liberian settlers. The history of Liberia shows the commonwealth era (1822–1846) as characterized by a struggle on the one hand between the settlers from America and the indigenous people. On the other hand another struggle was occurring between the settlers and the European slave traders and expansionists in West Africa. The struggle continued on both fronts. By the time independence was declared on July 26, 1847, the slave trade was almost abolished; but the task of integration was still a long way from being complete.

Failing to form a convincingly inclusive government of settlers and the indigenous population, the settlers wrangled among themselves first as "mulattos and dark-skinned" and later as "Congos and Americo-Liberians," the "Congos" being those who did not arrive in Liberia from America but were settled in Liberia from slave ships seized off the West African coast while being taken to be sold as slaves. Even as a two-party state between 1847 and the 1940's, the contest remained among the settlers themselves, excluding the indigenous people. The True Whig Party (TWP) was, to a large extent, responsible for the emergence of a one-party state in Liberia after the election of President William V. S. Tubman. Under the leadership of President Tubman, several notable achievements were recorded. They included an improved socieconomic environment and a policy of integration that sought to promote national unity. However, Tubman was known for either buying out his opponents through a system of patronage or shutting them out through threats, intimidations, and imprisonment.

The unification and integration policy of Tubman was designed to create a social and political situation that transcended ethnicity. There seems to have been a controlled system of absorbing a limited number of indigenous persons into the mainstream of national life. The results of the unification and integration policy were unconvincing to many who saw it as perpetuating Americo-Liberian rule and pacifying the indigenous population. When Tubman died in 1971 after twenty-seven unbroken years in office and was succeeded by Tolbert, discontent began to rise.

A group of Liberian intellectuals who became known as "the Progressives" launched a campaign not only to remove Tolbert as president but particularly to change the political face of Liberia. The Progressives began advocating a political philosophy with a socialist-communist ring. The Tolbert government saw the movement as socialist; but not being used to opposition, the government did not know what to do. The Progressives targeted the ordinary masses and used grassroots organizations to effect their policies. The message the Progressives were getting across was not powersharing but a total change that wanted to see indigenous Liberians in total control. Today some claim that the major purpose of their political activism was to introduce a multiparty system; unfortunately, while they achieved it, there were more dangerous ramifications.

Using such slogans as, "Monkey Work, Baboon Draw" and "In the Cause of the People," the settlers and the indigenous citizens were pitted against one another. The pressure groups in Liberia compared the country to South Africa during the apartheid days. An economic picture of Liberia was painted where the impression was given that with Liberia's 2.5 million population and its gross national product (GNP) of over 25 million dollars, each Liberian could get 1 million dollars per year. Agricultural and developmental projects like SUSUKUU strengthened the cooperative spirit of the ordinary Liberian and impressed upon the people that Liberia could be better off than it was at the time. The message was strong and the ends were just; however, the Progressives did not want to wait for social change to take effect; since gradualism was not the plan, the means they employed became questionable because of the results.

Grassroots support for the Progressives increased dramatically. Using local organizations, mass meetings, mass education, and mass media, by 1979 the plan of the Progressives was consolidated; all they needed was some instability. The government played into their hands. Instead of dealing with the persons involved in the Progressive movement, the national leadership responded by attacking the opposition as proponents of socialism and communism, declaring these systems as alien to Liberia. The high level of illiteracy and semi-literacy in Liberia made the masses susceptible to the propaganda.

Then the government erred by raising the price of rice, Liberia's staple food, from $21.00 to $24.00 (until 1985, the US dollar was legal tender in Liberia). This move was resisted by the Progressives. First they declared that rice could be obtained for far less than what the government was selling it for; second, they mobilized the people and staged a demonstration on April 14, 1979. The government called on the army to stop the demonstration; and in the process of trying to break up the crowd, a riot broke out. Many persons were wounded and a few persons died. Unable to predict the next few days and testing the recently signed mutual defense and nonaggression treaty of the Mano River Union, to which Liberia, Guinea, and Sierra Leone were signatories, Tolbert called upon the Guinean government to provide troops to protect Monrovia.

The tension subsided while the Guinean troops patrolled Monrovia. But like a volcano, the rumblings of discontent continued. A successful OAU summit was held that year; 1980, the following year, brought a reversal of events. In a miscalculated move to stamp out once and for all the opposition that had framed itself into the Progressive People's Party (PPP) and the Movement for Justice in Africa (MOJA), the Tolbert government arrested leaders of the opposition. Whether these rumors were true or not, some persons felt the government's major concern was the methods employed by the opposition to destabilize the country with no thought of the aftermath; others felt the government's reaction was to maintain itself in power.

The dramatic change finally came on April 12, 1980, when the Tolbert government was overthrown. Tolbert himself was killed and a military government, named and styled the "People's Redemption Council" (PRC), was ushered into power. The new government was led by Master Sergeant Samuel K. Doe as the head of state and was composed of seventeen enlisted men of the Armed Forces of Liberia (AFL). A quick roundup of cabinet ministers, legislators, and other government officials was made. Thirteen of those officials were executed publicly after being tried by a special military tribunal. Most of those appointed in the new government were Progressives and many were inducted into the army with rank.

Although the PRC claimed it came to power because of rampant corruption and misuse of public office, among other charges, the more serious message that came out of the new government was that the era of Americo-Liberian domination was over and it was now time for the indigenous Liberians to exercise power. The song the masses danced to in the streets was, "Congo woman born rogue, Country woman born soldier." The actions and policies of the government in the first few months showed that Americo-Liberians were clearly the target. Their properties were seized, many were jailed, and several slogans against them could be heard. Only later were token attempts made to encourage Americo-Liberian participation in the military government of the PRC. The reason for encouraging this participation may have been that most of those appointed to high-ranking positions were without training, experience, or education and were most incapable of running the government. It also may have been that those in high-ranking positions were made aware of the dangers of going to the extreme by isolating the Americo-Liberians.

During the years following, something went seriously wrong among members of the PRC. It seemed one ethnic group wanted to exercise greater control over the others; when there was disagreement over policies, it was interpreted as undermining the interest of the government. One by one, Doe began eliminating members of the PRC, several of whom were accused of plotting coups and were subsequently executed. The most serious disagreement seemed to have been between Doe, a Krahn from southeastern Liberia, and Thomas Quiwonkpa, a Gio from Nimba in northern Liberia, another member of the PRC. The story that circulated was that Doe wanted to continue in power through elections although the PRC had promised to return the country to civilian rule after a period of military leadership. Quiwonkpa encouraged Doe and the rest of the PRC members to be faithful to the mandate of the coup; this was misunderstood by Doe. Quiwonkpa was isolated, demoted in rank, and sent to the ministry of defense as chief of staff.

As though this action against Quiwonkpa did not satisfy Doe, he directed an organized plan to suppress Quiwonkpa's ethnic group in northern Liberia. In 1984, the Armed Forces of Liberia (AFL) staged an infamous act known as the "Nimba Raid," killing scores of people in Nimba County, burning villages, torturing others, and forcing hundreds more to flee into exile, including Quiwonkpa himself. That same year, the University of Liberia, the breeding ground of the Progressives who were increasingly opposed to Doe's leadership, came under attack. After some lecturers and students were arrested and imprisoned, the students resisted by staging a boycott of classes. This made Doe very angry. He ordered his defense minister, Gray D. Allison, who was later tried and convicted for ritualistic murder, to tell the students to "move or be removed" from the campus. This the AFL did, resulting in the rape, torture, arrest, and even murder of students. Many persons became disenchanted with Doe because, though he was an indigenous president that was thought would be better for Liberia, he had dashed the hopes of a large number of people. Some claim that nowhere in the history of the country, despite its failures and problems, had such atrocities ever occurred with complete disregard for the lives of the people. Others argue that Doe did in ten years what the warring factions did in less time. Suffice it to say that the decades of the 1980's and the 1990's were stormy years of extreme trials and tribulations for the nation.

General and presidential elections were scheduled for 1985 and the National Democratic Party of Liberia (NDPL) was organized by Doe. By this time the friendship that existed between the Progressives and the military government had turned sour. It had become obvious that Doe wanted to change the beat of the drum they (the PRC) danced into power with and to develop some ideas of his own. One of those ideas was becoming president of the Second Republic and perpetuating himself in power for life. A good number of civilians recruited by the PRC left government service; some fled the country, while others remained in Liberia and organized their own political parties.

One of the plans of the various parties to vote Doe out of office was to form a coalition. Five parties joined forces; they included the Liberia Action Party (LAP), the Liberia Unification Party (LUP), the Unity Party (UP), the United People's Party (UPP), and the Liberia People's Party (LPP). This coalition obviously frightened Doe and the NDPL. Doe quickly threatened them with arrest for plots he believed they had fabricated. Some of the leaders of the coalition were arrested and detained. To ease the tension the Liberian Council of Churches (LCC) quickly became involved as peacemaker. After several sessions of mediation, the NDPL and the coalition agreed to create an atmosphere that would make the elections free and fair.

Nobody will really know the true results of the October 1985 elections except the Special Elections Commission (SECOM) headed by a veteran diplomat, Ambassador Emmett Harmon. Following the day of voting, Liberian television showed scenes of burned ballot papers and delayed return of ballot boxes. Reports told of ballot papers and boxes that disappeared. Despite these irregularities, it still came as no surprise when the results were announced and Doe was declared the winner. Some joked that the total number of votes exceeded the population of Liberia. Though disgruntled, the coalition accepted the results.

During the early morning hours of November 12, 1985, Thomas Quiwonkpa, who had fled Liberia the year before, returned and seized power from Doe. Unfortunately, this adventure was short-lived as Doe returned to power on the same day. The mayhem and carnage that followed were indescribable as the AFL systematically sought out people for elimination. Every county felt the effect; but Nimba, Quiwonkpa's home, suffered the most. Quiwonkpa himself was later arrested and brutally slaughtered.

Doe was inducted into office the following January, but the witch hunting did not stop. From 1986 to 1990, the government unleashed a reign of terror on the people of Liberia. Unwarranted arrests, detentions without trials, mysterious disappearances, and gruesome deaths characterized the era.

Contrary to the belief of some that the church lost moral authority during the Doe regime, the church remained the only morally authoritative voice. The government openly criticized, ridiculed, and derided the church, hoping to make it powerless. The government went further and withdrew duty-free privileges and suspended subsidies to church-related health and educational institutions. This action on the part of the government forced some church-related educational institutions to close; but, on the whole, it actually boosted the ministries of the churches by stimulating increased overseas support.

Not only did the government of Liberia under President Doe attack the church through its institutions, it also targeted pastors and church leaders. Doe threatened to publicly flog any pastor or bishop who preached against the evil practices of his regime. However, none of the charges trumped up against the church withstood scrutiny and soon, sensing he was barking up the wrong tree, Doe began to seek out the church for advice, which he never followed.

It is hard to name a single factor that was responsible for the outbreak of the war; probably it was a combination of elements that led to the civil crisis. Given the tumultuous flow of events during the 1980's, it came as no surprise to many when war erupted.

The rumor of the December 24, 1989, attack by the National Patriotic Front of Liberia (NPFL) trickled into Monrovia and Butuo, from where the first offensive was launched. All doubts as to the authenticity of the story were removed when, in an interview with the BBC (British Broadcasting Corporation), Charles Taylor confirmed the rumors and claimed the leadership of the NPFL. The government of Liberia tried to allay the fears of the citizens by claiming that the uprising would be brought under control.

The rapid advance of the rebels and the frequent defeat of the government forces in the rural areas became evident from reports in the local papers. A war of words ensued between Taylor and Doe. Doe accused Taylor of being a fugitive wanted in Liberia for embezzling millions of dollars belonging to the government of Liberia. While in the United States, Taylor had been arrested and detained in a Massachusetts prison awaiting extradition to Liberia but managed to escape. Taylor denied Doe's charges, saying he was falsely accused and Doe was only trying to tarnish his reputation.

After leaving the United States, Taylor traveled to areas where he met other Liberian dissidents, mainly people from Nimba County and those of Americo-Liberian stock. The exiles from Nimba were seeking revenge for the death of General Quiwonkpa and for the destruction of their villages and families. The Americo-Liberians wanted revenge for the deaths of President Tolbert and the thirteen men executed during the early days of the 1980 coup and for other atrocities committed against them by the Doe regime.

Doe, being the common enemy of a number of groups, served as the common denominator uniting the dissidents. Too many persons and possibly some nations wanted Doe out of the way. Reports indicated that Libya served as the training ground with support coming from Ivory Coast where the late President Houphouet Boigny was vindictive against Doe for the death of his son-in-law, A. Benedict Tolbert, son of the late Liberian president, William Richard Tolbert, Jr.

Though the war began hundreds of miles away from the capital, Doe and his supporters felt that Taylor had support in Monrovia. Doe tried some pacifying moves to calm the storm. He granted political clemency to about seventy-five political prisoners and lifted the ban imposed on two newspapers, *Footprints* and *Suntimes*. He also lifted a ban on the Roman Catholic radio station, ELCM. Doe met with citizens of Nimba County, tried to reconcile their differences, and urged them not to support Taylor and the NPFL. Despite Doe's pleas, the NPFL continued its advance toward Monrovia and its assault on Monrovia.

As security forces in Monrovia tried to locate supporters of the Front in Monrovia, the Gio and Mano residents became prime targets of Doe's "death squads" that roamed the streets of Monrovia after curfew, which was 6:00 P.M. Each morning, bodies were found in various parts of the city, while other persons disappeared mysteriously and were never found. Out of fear for their lives, Mano and Gio persons and those who felt threatened sought refuge at the United

Nations compound on Tubman Boulevard in Congo Town in May of 1990. On May 28, armed persons dressed in military uniforms raided the UN compound, killed a security person, wounded another, and abducted about thirty persons, none of whom was ever found. Doe visited the compound on the morning of the abduction and was booed by the survivors.

The experience was so horrifying that the survivors left the UN compound and sent a delegation to the Liberian Council of Churches (LCC) to inform them of their plight. The LCC, already in a meeting at the United Methodist Central Office, received the news with grave concern and agreed to provide shelter and protection for the displaced. Saint Peter's Lutheran Church was made available; and later, the S. Trowen Nagbe United Methodist Church, the Providence Baptist Church, and the Arthur Barclay Technical Institute of the Catholic Church housed the displaced, who included ordinary citizens, government officials, and other prominent citizens, all fleeing the wrath of President Samuel Doe and his government.

As the situation worsened, it became obvious that the Front was not only targeting Krahns; the Mandingoes, in Nimba County especially, were being killed allegedly because it was believed they were pointing out supporters of the Front in that county to government soldiers, thus showing their sympathy for the Doe government. Since the majority of the Mandingoes in Liberia are Muslims, and some of them were killed in mosques, efforts were made to avert the notion that Christians were killing Muslims. A part of this effort was to invite leaders of the Muslim community in Liberia to work with the Liberia Council of Churches; together they formed the Inter-Faith Mediation Committee (IFMC) to negotiate between the NPFL and the government of President Doe.

The formation of the IFMC was a major achievement that helped keep the war in Liberia from degenerating into a religious one. Since Muslims and Christians have coexisted peacefully in Liberia, it seemed practical that when it came to the issue of peace and Liberia's stability, both groups had to work together. Criticized by both conservative Christian and Muslim groups, one has to admit the IFMC made an impact on the nation with its contribution to the peace process.

During the first six months of the conflict, the IFMC met regularly to discuss what could be done to neutralize the situation. Regular visits were made to the Executive Mansion and to the Legislature, opening a line of communication to the NPFL leadership.

The IFMC came up with a plan that was eventually used by ECOWAS in Liberia. The IFMC recommended that ECOWAS send troops to Liberia to maintain law and order and to keep the conflicting parties apart while discussions continued. The IFMC also included in its proposal the resignation of President Doe and the appointment of an interim government that would lead the country to elections scheduled for October, 1991. It was a major negotiating breakthrough when both the government of Liberia and the NPFL agreed to hold talks chaired by the IFMC to be conducted in Freetown, in neighboring Sierra Leone, at the American Embassy during the middle of June, 1990.

In order to add momentum and urgency to the peace talks, the IFMC called a "peace march" on Thursday, June 14, 1990, and requested all who wanted to see "an end to the wanton killings and the conflict in Liberia" to turn out and join the march. As the peace talks in Freetown began on Thursday, June 14, an unprecedented crowd of Liberians, hungry and yearning for peace, converged on the compound of the United Methodist Church (UMC) in Sinkor, Monrovia, for the march. The IFMC was not surprised at the level of turnout because there was a high level of fear, anxiety, and concern in the residents of Monrovia. Apart from the wanton massacres taking place regularly, a number of prominent Liberians were found killed in gruesome ways.

Bishop Arthur F. Kulah, the author of this book, led the march from the UMC compound. The march went without incident and flowed past the Executive Mansion where Doe lived and worked. We led the marchers to the American Embassy at Mamba Point, west of Monrovia. At the American Embassy, we were met on arrival by the US ambassador. We read a statement calling on the US government to intervene and stop the carnage. In response, the ambassador made it clear that the crisis was an internal matter and there would be no American intervention; this was a matter to be resolved by Liberians themselves. Disappointed but undaunted, the march continued to the executive pavilion on Ashmun where a worship service was held. Emotional expressions at this service were strong and tensions were high.

In Freetown, Sierra Leone, the peace talks were chaired by the president of the Liberian Council of Churches who also led the IFMC delegation. The issues were placed on the table. The NPFL insisted on the resignation of President Doe. The government of Liberia delegation, led by the justice minister, stated emphatically that President Doe would not resign but that he had agreed not to contest presidential elections scheduled for October, 1991. This offer was unacceptable to the Front. The first set of talks ended without any resolutions or agreement, but it was decided the discussions would continue.

In order to drive home the point that peace was the most urgent need, the IFMC organized another march on June 26. The second march also began from the UMC compound. Less than five blocks from the compound, the march was stopped by soldiers of the AFL who ordered the marchers not to travel near the Executive Mansion but to use another route. After a word of prayer, kneeling on the pavement in the open street, we took another route. This march, like the previous one, was to end in a worship service; in addition, a video documentary on the war in rural Liberia was to be shown. Near the worship hall, a group of marchers broke away from the main group and went toward the ministry of defense, chanting anti-Doe slogans. The security forces eventually broke up the crowd, and the day ended in confusion.

Two days later, the political parties and pressure groups planned a third march. This march began at a location where the marchers did not have to go past the Executive Mansion. During this march, government soldiers fired their guns into the air to disperse the crowd. Pandemonium broke out; the crowd went wild and ran in all directions; a number of persons were wounded; and the march ended abruptly, which increased the tension.

The marches and talks were all part of a larger plan to influence the parties to the conflict to end the war. The local efforts described above were buttressed by international attempts to negotiate a peaceful settlement. Unfortunately, it seems both sides wanted to prove a point and had enough antagonism for each other to reject well-meaning efforts. The battle was to the end.

On July 2, 1990, the NPFL attached and captured the suburb of Paynesville just outside of Monrovia. Apparently the Front was too close to final victory to attend any more peace talks. Things were getting desperate; so was the government. Everybody was a target. Religious and political leaders went into hiding as death squads sought out persons believed to be enemies of the Doe regime. No one was safe. The legal system collapsed, the medical institutions struggled to meet the needs, and there was no law and order. The full impact of the war could be felt in Monrovia; total anarchy reigned.

In mid-July, the Lutheran church that served as the sanctuary for hundreds of displaced persons fearing for their lives was attacked by armed persons believed to be government soldiers. Over six hundred persons were slaughtered in cold blood. Displaced persons across the street from the Lutheran church in the S. Trowen Nagbe United Methodist Church took to the streets and were hunted like animals. Liberia had reached its lowest point.

But the people of Liberia were not about to give up. The next set of discussions was held in Banjul, the capital of Gambia, another West African state. It was agreed at these meetings that an interim government would be set up. Dr. Amos C. Sawyer, dean of Liberia College of the University of Liberia and professor of political science, was elected by Liberians present at that meeting to head the interim government. Dr. Sawyer's election was later confirmed and ratified by the All Liberian Conference held in March 1991 at the Monrovia City Hall.

Meanwhile, the carnage and the bloodshed continued. The leaders of West Africa, particularly President Ibrahim

Babangida of Nigeria, were moved at the plight of Liberia and agreed they could not sit idly and watch the destruction of another West African nation. Not only would it be immoral to do so, but the political implications were far-reaching. Under the leadership of Nigeria, the ECOWAS Peace Monitoring Group (ECOMOG) was organized. ECOMOG troops arrived in Monrovia on August 24, 1990, Liberia's Flag Day. While attempting to disembark at the Freeport of Monrovia, the ECOMOG troops came under attack from the NPFL. Fighting their way to shore, they landed and quickly established themselves as a force to be reckoned with.

By this time, the NPFL had experienced a splinter resulting in the formation of the Independent National Patriotic Front of Liberia (INPFL) led by General Prince Y. Johnson. Taylor and the NPFL controlled the eastern section of Monrovia and the rest of the country; the INPFL dominated northern Monrovia, including Bushrod Island and the Settlement of Caldwell, which became Johnson's military base.

A relationship quickly developed between President Doe and General Johnson. The friendship seemed cordial, but it was a dangerous one. Johnson visited Doe at the Barclay Training Center barracks, a formidable barracks built by the Tubman administration to protect the Executive Mansion, which Taylor tried to capture several times, to no avail. Accordingly, both Doe and Johnson had agreed that Taylor was the common enemy and that, upon informing the other beforehand, they could exchange visits.

Unfortunately, President Doe made the unpardonable mistake of going to the Freeport of Monrovia on Bushrod Island, which was manned by Johnson and the INPFL, without letting Johnson know. Johnson, known for his erratic behavior, asked Doe whether he, Johnson, was informed and therefore aware of Doe's visit to the Freeport. No amount of reasoning helped; and in a sudden burst of anger, Doe was shot in the legs and eventually, after being tortured, was killed and buried, some say at Johnson's Caldwell base while others claim at the Island Clinic.

With the death of Doe, Dr. Amos Sawyer was flown in and

inducted into office by the Chief Justice of Liberia as President of the Interim Government of National Unity (IGNU). President Sawyer made early attempts to establish civil authority, made human welfare services functional, set up the legal system, and created a semblance of civilization, law, order, and democracy.

It was expected that Taylor, having contributed to the fall of Doe—something he claimed was his primary objective—would end the war. To the shock, dismay, and disappointment of many, the war continued. Taylor evidently wanted more than just getting rid of Doe; he wanted the presidency. Many persons believe that if Taylor had abandoned his plans to take the presidency by force and contest the elections earlier than he did, he would have won easily, because he was very popular with the people.

Sawyer attempted to secure a cease-fire and to effect disarmament, demobilization, and rehabilitation of the fighters of both the NPFL and the INPFL—elections were the ultimate goal. Sawyer himself had agreed, as a part of the peace plan, that he would not contest the elections as a presidential candidate. In order to achieve this, conferences were held in Yamoussokro, Ivory Coast, and ranged from Yamoussokro I–IV for the number of conferences held there. Nothing substantial materialized from these meetings. Whatever agreements were reached were soon broken by the NPFL leadership based on some trivial and frivolous reasons justifying why Taylor had signed but could not uphold the agreement.

As a result of these talks, ECOMOG deployed its troops in various parts of Liberia to begin building confidence among the people. An insider hinted that on a fateful day, a group of Senegalese soldiers stationed in Vahun, Lofa County, went to the market. When they arrived at the market, NPFL soldiers in the area attempted to disarm them, but they resisted. An exchange of gunfire erupted. Most of the Senegalese soldiers retreated to their base, but six were not able to return. Allowing them to use their ammunition until it ran out, the NPFL fighters surrounded the Senegalse, arrested them, and took them to Gbarnga. Some say Taylor personally ordered their execution.

The field commander of ECOMOG at the time was considered most ineffective. When the six Senegalese soldiers were killed, ECOMOG offered no response; not even a squadron of fighter planes flew over the NPFL territory as a warning. It was speculated that this field commander did not really come to Liberia to bring peace.

The NPFL disdained President Sawyer because it felt the interim presidency belonged to Mr. Taylor; consequently it was believed there were attempts to assassinate President Sawyer. Because of this highly held belief, particularly among the security personnel and government officials in Monrovia, President Sawyer declined to attend a summit of the two leaders in Harbel, Firestone Plantations Company, a meeting I was instrumental in arranging. Needless to say, this action on the part of President Sawyer brought disappointment to all Liberians who had prayed and longed for peace.

One of the strengths of the NPFL at the time, and remained up to the point of this meeting, was a well-organized propaganda mechanism that transmitted information and sometimes misinformation to the people of Liberia and the world. Using the radio and newspaper, the NPFL succeeded in educating, informing, and at times brainwashing those in the hinterland about ECOMOG being an occupying force; the people developed an abhorrence and contempt for ECOMOG.

There were outstanding personalities and some world leaders who also succeeded in getting the international governments to believe that Major Taylor had good intentions and that, indeed, he was the persecuted, not the persecutor. While efforts were made to produce something positive and really accept the fact that Taylor meant well, the NPFL launched "Operation Octopus" against the city of Monrovia. The Front used ground forces to storm the outskirts of Monrovia, especially where there were swamps. They abducted hundreds of civilians and forced them to the NPFL-held territory, many of whom died along the way or were killed. Rockets were thrown into Monrovia from all directions and many persons lost their lives as a result. ECOMOG had superiority over the Front both on the ground and in the air and could have neutralized the NPFL between October and December, 1992. Inside sources suggested that ECOMOG came within reach of capturing Taylor, but the IGNU did not allow it to keep room for discussions open and allow Taylor to "save face."

Accordingly, pre-empting "Operation Octopus," the IGNU facilitated the training of an elite force called the "Black Berets" to work along with ECOMOG. Though the interim government of Dr. Sawyer was criticized for this action, it is believed he was vindicated, as one of his aides put it, by the performance of the Black Berets during and after "Operation Octopus."

Some argued that "Operation Octopus" raised the need for additional military pressure on the NPFL. The result was the formation of the United Liberation Movement for Democracy in Liberia (ULIMO). Reports have it that Dr. Sawyer pressured the NPFL militarily to abandon its empty dream of conquest by force. Within a short period of time, ULIMO's presence was seen and felt in Monrovia.

Soon it became clear that the leaders of ULIMO had ulterior motives and a hidden agenda. The main organizers of ULIMO were from the Krahn and Mandingo ethnic groups, staunch supporters of the Doe government. The organization did not exist long before a serious rift developed within it. It seemed one of the organizers, Alhaji Kromah, a Muslim-Mandingo and a former close confidant of Doe, wanted to exercise more influence than the others. Apparently, the Krahns did not like the idea of a Mandingo controlling what they believed was their organization. The rift resulted in a schism, and two organizations emerged—one was ULIMO-K for Kromah and the Mandingo-Muslims while the other, ULIMO-J, was controlled by General Roosevelt Johnson and the Krahns.

After taking Tubmanburg, Bomi County, in northwestern Liberia from the NPFL, which they used as their military base, the two groups fought viciously to oust the other. ULIMO-J overpowered ULIMO-K, forcing them to flee the area and retreat into nearby Lofa County, further northwest near the Guinean border. The atrocities committed by the

ULIMO-K forces while fleeing their rivals and seeking to establish themselves in Lofa County prompted the citizens of Lofa to form what became known as the Lofa Defense Force (LDF). Its major purpose was to protect and defend Lofa land and citizens, according to the organizers.

The rationale of protecting and defending the land and citizens was the basis of not only the LDF but also another warring faction formed by the people of southeastern Liberia, especially Sinoe and Grand Gedeh counties. The Liberia Peace Council (LPC) was led by Dr. George Boley. All these pressure forces emerged as a result of the infamous "Operation Octopus" by local people to stop the NPFL and protect their areas. It is hard to say what would have happened if each region had produced its own citizen defense force to drive out the NPFL. All these warring factions, as they later came to be called, ended up being parties to the conflict and earned bargaining powers as they were subsequently invited to attend and participate in peace conferences on Liberia.

"Operation Octopus" complicated the peace process and created more mistrust among Liberians. Even I, as bishop of the United Methodist Church, the largest Protestant denomination in Liberia, was persecuted unjustly. In my attempt to get both sides to keep talking, and feeling an obligation to stay in touch with United Methodists all over Liberia, I made regular visits throughout the country. This was misunderstood by many who saw my visits to "Greater Liberia," the area under Taylor's control, as sympathy and support for Taylor; thus they branded me "The Rebel Bishop." The fighters of the NPFL also saw me as a spy for the "other side" and even had a warrant out for my life. During "Operation Octopus," while enroute to my residence from central Monrovia, I was detained at an ECOMOG checkpoint, taken from my jeep, and made to sit on the pavement as the crowd jeered at me. Despite the misunderstanding and disgrace, time has proven me to be a true peacemaker whose good intentions contributed to the dawning of peace in Liberia.

In 1994, another peace conference on Liberia was held in Cotonou, Benin, also in West Africa. During this conference, it was decided that the parties to the conflict be represented in the interim government if there was to be a genuine peace in Liberia. It was argued that since the warring factions held the guns, they would be in a better position to usher in a new day for Liberia. The Liberian National Transitional Government (LNTG) was formed in Cotonou with a five-person collective presidency known as the Council of State (COS). The warring factions nominated persons for the cabinet, the judiciary, and the legislature.

One of President Sawyer's points of contention was that before a new government could be installed, disarmament must be in process. The Cotonou Accord said that the installation of the LNTG would take place "concomitantly" with disarmament. The word *concomitant* caused such a big stir that President Sawyer was accused of trying to maintain himself in power. Eventually, the idea of "concomitant" was dropped. In the cause of peace, Dr. Sawyer agreed to step down; and the LNTG, under the chairmanship of a lawyer, Professor David D. Kpormakpor, was inaugurated. On the Council of State were representatives of the NPFL, ULIMO, LPC, and the civilians of Liberia whose representative was nominated by the outgoing Interim Government of National Unity (IGNU).

During its tenure, the LNTG I, as it came to be called later, made some efforts toward disarmament. A system was set in motion in which fighters of the various warring factions were to be disarmed, demobilized, and rehabilitated; the program was supported by ECOWAS, the United Nations, and friendly governments, with funds set aside as a "Peace Fund" by Chairman Kpormakpor. Unfortunately, most of the money was expended; as yet, no proper accounting has been given to the Liberian people as to how that money was spent. The disarmament results of the LNTG I were far from encouraging. The lack of integrity and accountability have been the plagues of the last two transitional governments because those nominated to public office had no commitment to the peace process and were only interested in acquiring wealth. Many of these new fictional officials were not even knowledgeable of their functions in government and public corporations. They seemed to be rewarded because they fought against the people of Liberia.

One of the explanations given for the slow progress toward peace was the absence of principals on the Council of State. As it was, the representatives on the Council had to consult their leaders regularly before major decisions were taken. This caused a problem in moving the peace process forward, or so it was argued.

Another meeting on Liberia was called in Akosombo, Ghana, where the decision was reached that in order to effect the peace plan and institute civilian rule, the leaders of the warring factions themselves would become members of the Council of State. The Liberian National Transitional Government II (LNTG II) was formed, the number of members on COS increased to six. These six members were comprised of a civilian chairperson, a traditional chief in the person of Tamba Tailor, a civilian representative, and a representative each from the NPFL, ULIMO, and LPC. The civilian representative was elected by the Liberia National Conference under my supervision as chairman of the LNC's elections commission: Oscar Quiah emerged victorious. Professor Wilton Sankawulo, an English professor at the University of Liberia, was selected to chair the Council; Charles Taylor represented the NPFL, Alhaji Kromah went in for ULIMO, while George Boley was the LPC representative.

The hopes of the Liberian people were raised once more. With the warring factions on the Council of State, nothing could go wrong. By this time, the people of Liberia were ready. The stage was set. The decision taken in Ghana was ratified in Nigeria. All that was needed was positive action.

TWO

FROM JOY TO SORROW

AVING explored the foundations and circumstances of the war, we now turn our attention to the presence of the leaders of the warring factions as part of the government of Liberia, what their coming did for the city of Monrovia, and the implications thereof.

Six months following the induction of the Liberia National Transitional Government I, the chairman of the Council of State, Professor David D. Kpormakpor openly admitted that the five-person collective presidency was a "mess." This probably explains why there were few results on the part of LNTG I to achieve disarmament and set the electoral process into motion as stipulated in the Abuja Accord. The entire game was a factional affair and a scramble for jobs.

Under LNTG I each factional representative pursued its interest in nominating those loyal to its leaders. Those appointed to responsible positions spent less time seeking the development and the welfare of the nation. On the contrary, there was a tendency to accrue wealth in usually unscrupulous ways knowing that the rapid change of appointments could see one in a position for only a short time.

Worst of all, the resources of the country remained under the control of the factions, especially the NPFL, ULIMO, and the LPC, which continued to become rich at the expense of the Liberian people. They made little attempt to improve the standards of living of the people. State-owned facilities declined and civil servants' salaries were delayed for months, reminiscent of the Doe era. Public schools were in rundown, dilapidated conditions while government hospitals and clinics suffered from a lack of drugs and other necessary supplies. Fortunately, health NGO's (nongovernmental organizations) like *Medicines sans Frontiere*, the Red Cross, and others came to the rescue of the people of Liberia. The only source of income and revenue during most of the war era was the Maritime Fund due to Liberia's large shipping registry; but the government squandered the money as soon as it was received.

All these problems and more prompted the discussion and decision that the major actors and "principal players" should be on the State Council. At conferences in Ghana and Nigeria, the discussions were not dominated by effective methods implementing disarmament and conducting elections; rather, the most pressing issues were who would get what ministries and public corporations, as it became obvious that certain government ministries and public corporations carried specific authority from which the overseeing faction would benefit. This situation showed a shift in focus from the primary objectives and priorities of national interest to the secondary concerns of a personal, selfish nature. Perhaps there was never really a concern for national interest.

The ordinary Liberian, tired of the war and yearning for peace, was ready to accept another chance. For most Liberians, the guiding adage was, "Where there is life, there is hope," and to keep hope alive is to believe that an opportunity for better times will one day come. The factions moved toward peace like wheels stuck in the mud. Their snail-paced actions were leading the nation nowhere but in circles. Still, Liberians hoped, fasted, and continued to pray.

The announcement that LNTG II would include the leaders of the warring factions on the Council of State brought sighs of relief. The warring factions had fought one another for five years up to that point, so many people believed their willingness to serve on the State Council meant they had some ideas or a political platform to make Liberia a better country. Therefore, the people of Liberia allowed them to come into power and put these ideas and plans to work for the good and the welfare of the nation and its people.

During the discussions in Ghana and Nigeria about the role of LNTG I, three of Charles Taylor's major nominees to the ministries of justice, internal affairs, and labor, Laveli Supuwood, Samuel Dokie, and Thomas Woewiyu respectively, defected from the National Patriotic Front of Liberia (NPFL). In public press conferences, they denounced Taylor and told the Liberian people not to trust him because his plan for the nation was devious and destructive. They went further to discuss their own roles in the war and asked the Liberian people to forgive them. Today, the three men remain active in the political life of the country, but not as NPFL members. Mr. Woewiyu founded a breakaway group known as the Central Revolutionary Council (NPFL-CRC), Mr. Supuwood remained active in the legal system serving as an associate justice of the Supreme Court and eventually as the presidential candidate for the Liberia Unification Party (LUP). These three men also seem to have become religious. Two of them have established a church known as Rock Church International that has a school connected with it.

But their confession took many by surprise. The three men had been staunch supporters of Taylor and the Front and had previously spoken vehemently and passionately for the Front and its cause. Some NPFL insiders attested that Woewiyu was one of the main architects and strategists of the NPFL war plans and combat actions.

For most people, Woewiyu, Dokie, and Supuwood had been with the Front too long and had done too much damage; so at the onset of their defection, it was hard for most people to take them seriously. Their motives were questioned and many persons refused to make them feel innocent or even forgiven. To show their disgust for Taylor and the NPFL, Woewiyu and a few others who sided with him organized the National Patriotic Front of Liberia—Central Revoluntiary Council (NPFL-CRC).

While Taylor and the other factional leaders were in Abuja, Nigeria, signing the final accord that would bring LNTG II into power, the NPFL-CRC allied itself with ULIMO-K and the LPC and attacked Gbarnga in September of 1994. Gbarnga was known as Taylor's stronghold and had the reputation of being "fortified" and "invincible." The "Fall of Gbarnga," as it known today, was a devastating military and psychological blow to the Front. It is believed some of Taylor's trusted men betrayed the Front and exposed it to danger. The NPFL-CRC, ULIMO-K, and the LPC attacked Gbarnga from all sides, took the city, and went on a revenge spree. Those who survived tell horrifying and terrifying stories of the "Fall of Gbarnga." The city has never really recovered from it, and the incident has been a stigma on the Front.

Taylor returned from Abuja, mobilized his men, and recaptured Gbarnga in a dramatic way, sending a message to Thomas Woewiyu, Alhaji Kromah, and George Boley that he was still in control of the Front and that the NPFL still possessed military powers. The "Fall of Gbarnga" did very little to dampen the enthusiasm and hopes of the people of Monrovia for peace. Liberians tended to be apathetic when one area of the country was attacked because, as some put it, every area of the country has to be hit so that everybody will feel the scourge of war. The long years of war have made the people of Liberia callous and take life for granted. Dead bodies lying in the streets tend to mean little or nothing to the average Liberian, and even children have come to view these dead bodies as a normal part of life. People threaten each other all the time, and the law of the nation tends to be the "law of survival." This is a dangerous sign of a nation in moral and social decline. For these reasons the news of the coming of LNTG II with the leaders of the warring factions on the Council of State was good news for the Liberian people—they were ready for peace.

One by one, the members of the State Council began to arrive in Monrovia. Kromah and Boley had been in Monrovia at various times, but coming as members of the Council of State brought joy to the hearts of many. Oscar Quiah was hailed as the civilian representative elected at the LNC. Chief Tamba Tailor arrived quietly. Professor Wilton Sankawulo was already living in Monrovia; he was flown to Abuja, confirmed as chairman of the State Council, and returned to Monrovia without ceremony or fanfare. The other two leaders of warring factions, Roosevelt Johnson of ULIMO-J and Francois Massaquoi, were appointed to head the ministry of rural development and the ministry of youth and sports, respectively.

None of the warring faction leaders received the euphoric and exhilarated reception that Charles Taylor did. When Taylor arrived, the normal life of the city came to a halt, and people lined the streets almost nine miles from the ECOMOG/NPFL buffer zone outside the city to downtown Monrovia. Taylor's arrival aroused jubilation among the residents of Monrovia. Probably the thousands of people who came to welcome Taylor did not do so out of love for the man but from a desire for peace and stability. A good number of persons turned out to catch a glimpse of the man who had held the country hostage. It was even rumored that hundreds of those who lined the streets of Monrovia cheering Taylor's arrival had been sent to Monrovia from Gbarnga by truckloads weeks before for this purpose.

Taylor was seen as a charismatic leader whose command of words and smooth talking ability convinced even the most serious antagonist. To many, Taylor was the hero who aroused courage; to others, he was the villain who stirred fear and masterminded the destruction of Liberia. To yet others he was a liberator, a revolutionary ready to lead Liberia into the twenty-first century, while others vowed to make life unpleasant for the warlords and their cronies. Taylor was loved and hated, worshiped and detested, adored and abhorred.

Speakers at the induction ceremony had words of hope and caution. The leaders of Liberia were encouraged by all to put their country first and end the suffering of their people. They were reminded that history would judge them harshly if they failed to lead their nation out of the valleys of war to the hills of peace. Nothing was expected to go wrong.

After years of death and destruction, it was hoped that the

people who had come to detest the word *warlords* would let these words sink into them and make a difference; but it was like "wasting water on ducks' backs." Six months after their induction as members of the Council of State of the Liberian National Transitional Government (LNTG II), life became more difficult for the people of Monrovia. Inflation continued to rise, salaries were delayed for longer periods of time, and the people became desperate. The leaders of the warring factions actually came to Monrovia to continue and even enhance the economic war against their own people. They continued to mine and sell gold and diamonds and to export rubber and timber, yet the nation's revenue-generating capacity did not improve. The minute increase came through the efforts of then-Finance Minister Wilson Tarpeh who tried tapping the few resources he could gain access to. Tarpeh made several meaningful attempts to strengthen the economy of Liberia; but each time funds came in, the government would spend them unwisely.

On the social level, the followers of the factional leaders who arrived in Monrovia with their bosses tried to move into certain areas of town. In the process, people were forcibly evicted from their homes and others were asked to leave if they lived in areas where some of the councilmen chose to reside because those neighborhoods had suddenly become "security zones." The bodyguards of some of the councilmen became reckless drivers, threatening the lives of pedestrians by their style of driving; they openly beat up people who questioned their actions.

When these erratic and irrational behaviors were questioned by journalists, politicians, and well-meaning residents of Monrovia, some were arbitrarily arrested and detained without appearing before a competent court of law. Monrovia became like the "wild west" during the early days of America; in the city, might made right—the rule of law became the survival of the fittest.

The cease-fire and disengagement of fighters from checkpoints as stipulated in the Abuja Accord were short-lived. The cease-fire was violated regularly. Even some members of the United Nations Observer Mission in Liberia (UNOMIL) were taken hostage from time to time. The warehouses of the United Nations and other relief agencies were constantly raided and looted by armed persons believed to be connected to the warring factions.

Slowly the hopes of the nation dissipated; discouragement and despondence set in. The social problems of prostitution, alcoholism, drug addiction, racketeering, smuggling, and other vices became more serious and moved to dangerous levels. The social and moral fabric of the nation that had started to come apart from the start of the war eroded even further; and even though churches and other religious organizations continued to minister more vigorously, their efforts were undermined by the lack of basic necessities.

ECOMOG soldiers have always been friends of Liberians. On one occasion, a Guinean ECOMOG friend came to see me at my home. He looked dejected and downhearted. When I asked him what was wrong, he told me that he and many of his peers were suffering from low morale. He said that when the warring faction leaders arrived in Monrovia, ECOMOG soldiers had high expectations for peace. But to him it seemed that whenever the country moved four steps forward, it moved six steps backward beyond where it was before.

Those of their group that worked closely with the Liberian leaders have realized that those in control were not interested in peace. Many ECOMOG soldiers, he lamented, "had little or no contact" with their families at home. "Could it be that the warring faction leaders were trying to wear them out so that they would withdraw and go home, thus leaving the warlords in complete control?" He did not have an answer to this question he raised, but I counseled with him and tried to cheer him up.

Coincidentally, not long afterward, I traveled to Buchanan City in Grand Bassa County along the coast for an Episcopal visit. During my visit there, I heard that my ECOMOG friend had been knocked down and killed by a vehicle. Such were the woes of frustration.

While in Buchanan City, a personal friend came to see me. As we talked about events in the country, he told me how extremely discouraged he was because of the absence of peace. He owned a farm not too far from Buchanan City; but because of the LPC's presence in the area, he could not go into his village without a military pass. Most of what he might try to bring back from his farm would be taken from him by the fighters. Sometimes these LPC fighters went into Buchanan City, created confusion, and sometimes even killed people with impunity.

In many ways, my two friends mentioned above summarized the general feelings of the people. Hope had turned to despair, glory became gloom, joy turned to sorrow. Once more the people had to sit and wait.

Some politicians and many of the Progressives, who facilitated the fall of the Tolbert government, were still present in Liberia, living in Monrovia. They began meeting to chart plans for elections. From what it seemed, some political parties were planning to form an alliance in order to defeat Taylor and his National Patriotic Party (NPP).

Taylor began having regular press conferences when the political pressure began to rise. He increased the number of press conferences from once a week to twice or more week, becoming open and direct in his attacks. He called the politicians and, if they overstepped their bounds, put them in their places. One of the politicians responded by challenging those they called "agents of death" to take the political race. Tensions began to rise because the warring faction leaders did not like suddenly being called "agents of death." The ministry of justice, which was under Taylor's control, began to act in an unjust manner. People would be invited to the ministry for discussions, and then they would be roughed up and/or jailed at the police station. The public became defiant, and some called the ministry of justice the "ministry of injustice." These acts of intimidation were believed to be designed to break the spirit of the few who dared stand up to Taylor and his threats.

In December of 1995, ECOMOG began deploying in parts of

Liberia as a part of the Abuja Accord. They deployed in areas controlled by the NPFL without any incidents. Then ECOMOG deployed in Tubmanburg, the stronghold of ULIMO-J and Major General Roosevelt Johnson. Shortly after ECOMOG deployed in Tubmanburg, fighters of ULIMO-J attacked them and seized some of their weapons.

The stories behind why the fighters of ULIMO-J attacked ECOMOG and seized some of their weapons varied. One story had it that when the ECOMOG high command changed the contingent already assigned in the area, ULIMO-J rejected the idea because they had already established a cordial relationship with the previously assigned contingent in Tubmanburg. Another version was that the newly assigned commander of ECOMOG in the area was unfriendly, did not allow much freedom of movement by ULIMO-J soldiers, and even harassed them. General Johnson, in a publication explaining the "events and causes" responsible for the tension in Bomi Hills, wrote that Nigerian battalions (NaBatt 17 and 22) were "engaged in shooting at ULIMO-J and have supported ULIMO-K." Whatever justification was given, it is clear that the attack on ECOMOG by Johnson's men was a dangerous move that changed the course of events. This action was now open to be used by anyone. ECOMOG quickly withdrew from Tubmanburg.

Negotiations to retrieve the weapons taken from ECOMOG got under way but yielded no fruitful results. Johnson justified his men's actions. As if the attack on ECOMOG was not enough, ULIMO-J attacked Kakata, forty-five miles from Monrovia, which was controlled by Taylor. The NPFL responded militarily and drove out ULIMO-J from Kakata. Their victory probably made the NPFL believe it was capable of greater military victories. This move by Taylor was unacceptable to the other warring factions and politicians, but Taylor likened the NPFL's action that of the US military intervention in some places without NATO.

By early 1996, the rift that had developed among the Council members was widening. A war of words ensued, and there were strong indications that a volcano would erupt. Yet some residents of Monrovia had enough faith in their self-imposed leaders that no matter how aggressive their words were, the people believed the leaders were too intelligent, had too much good will, and meant well enough to let Monrovia remain the safe haven that it was supposed to be.

The open exchange of words moved from Taylor and the politicians to between Kromah and Boley. Boley accused some members of the State Council of taking actions without the agreed consensus. He also accused others of exercising and overseeing responsibilities over ministries and agencies not under their control and of making appointments to positions not allotted to them. Meanwhile, the Johnson-ECOMOG incident in Tubmanburg was still haunting the government. The fear was that if ULIMO-J went without reprimand, it would be a dangerous precedent and would show that the government did not have the resolve to handle crises.

In response to the fracas, the government announced that General Roosevelt Johnson was suspended from his position as minister of rural development. In a matter of days, the high command of ULIMO-J issued a statement removing Johnson from his position as national chairman and replacing him with William Karyee. Another group of ULIMO-J fighters quickly issued a counter statement recognizing Johnson as their leader. Johnson's supporters were in the habit of stripping themselves naked and parading in public near his home. According to those familiar with the practices of the Krahn ethnic group to which Johnson belonged, this was one of the methods used to make voodoo or ju-ju to weaken the enemy. This uncivilized behavior represented public nuisance and disgrace.

One night in March, 1996, during a confrontation between ULIMO-J men loyal to Johnson and those loyal to Karyee, a fight broke out resulting in the death of a man connected with the Karyee group. The newspapers carried the stories and picture of the dead man for days.

The government openly invited General Johnson to the ministry of justice for a conference, after blaming him for the death of this person. Johnson refused to go; so an arrest warrant was issued for him. Johnson's men quickly came to his aid, kept him in his house, and patrolled the area. ECOMOG was put on alert and moved in a couple of armored tanks near Johnson's residence. By this time, given the nature of the press conferences, it was apparent that the rift within the government had become dangerously wide; little or no cohesion was left.

More and more Taylor became the spokesman for the government. Sankawulo was hardly heard and ended up being a figurehead chairman. Taylor invited the InterFaith Mediation Committee (IFMC) to speak with Johnson. The IFMC agreed and later understood that Taylor and the "government" expected the IFMC to hand-deliver Johnson to them to be arrested and tried for murder.

After meeting with Johnson, the IFMC learned from him that he would not turn himself in to be arrested because he had not committed any crime. It was true a man was killed near his place, but Johnson contended he did not kill the man and he could not be held responsible for the crime. Johnson further insisted that, if they wanted to try him, all warring faction leaders should be tried for war crimes.

When the IFMC made this known to the public, the newspapers grabbed the information and sensationalized it. This infuriated Taylor. Through his influence, Bishop Ronald Diggs of the Lutheran Church in Liberia and leader of the IFMC was arrested and taken to court on Wednesday of Holy Week, April 3, 1996. He was charged with obstruction of the flow of justice. The presiding judge, Bedell Fahn, allowed the placement of a thousand-dollar bail and scheduled the case for Friday, April 5. When the Christian leaders informed him that Friday was Good Friday, Judge Fahn responded, "Good Friday or Bad Friday, you are to appear before this court." It was later learned that the chairman of the State Council, Professor Sankawulo, had a personal grudge against Bishop Diggs dating back some fifteen years following his (Sankawulo's) seminary training when he was trying to enter the divine ministry of the Lutheran Church in Liberia. Sankawulo saw Diggs as the one who hindered his admission into the ministry of the church.

The charges against Diggs were later dropped, and the area in which General Johnson lived was declared "unsafe." Many of the residents in the area panicked, packed their belongings to leave, but had nowhere to go. Some, however, left their homes on Maundy Thursday, April 4. When they returned on Good Friday, April 5, most of their homes had been broken into, ransacked, and looted. This angered the residents who set roadblocks on Tubman Boulevard and refused to allow traffic through. The city became tense. During the afternoon, Taylor drove to the scene where the roadblocks had been set up. According to those who witnessed the exchange, the residents told Taylor they wanted a redress to their problems since they had nowhere to go following the looting of their homes. According to sources, Taylor assured them that the government would do everything possible to address their problems. He left and the roadblocks were removed.

That same day, the government announced that General Johnson was given until six o'clock that evening to turn himself in. Six o'clock came and Johnson did not turn himself in. It was anybody's guess as to what would happen next. The night was uneasy; so was everybody.

Early the next morning, on April 6 around three o'clock, gunfire rang out. Most people did not panic. About a year before, when Charles Julu, a former military strongman with Doe, had tried to stage a coup d'etat, he was smoked out of the Executive Mansion by ECOMOG in less than six hours. Maybe this was just another short-term military operation.

By seven that morning, the shooting was heavier and sounded more serious. From the episcopal residence where I live, I observed a flow of people with personal belongings tied up in bundles on their heads leaving the Sinkor area where Johnson lived, in Central Monrovia, going toward Paynesville, an eastern suburb.

I later learned that, during the night, men loyal to Taylor and Kromah had launched an offensive against Johnson's position. Throughout the day, the battle raged on. Taylor's radio station described the offensive as being lead by "government troops" seeking to bring Johnson to justice. Johnson's men were believed to have received assistance from the LPC and the AFL, most of whom were of the Krahn ethnic group as Johnson was. Early reports of the battle suggested that Johnson's men drove Taylor's men several blocks from the original point of attack toward Taylor's home. Johnson's men captured the airport and burned the terminal and an aircraft owned by the Weasua Air Transport, a local air transport company of a Spanish businessman.

During the afternoon, several trailers sixty to eighty feet long brought additional men belonging to the NPFL. The rumor was that Taylor had sent for fifteen thousand men belonging to his elite "marine" unit stationed at the military base known as "Eeala." It was an obvious sign that the war was escalating to dangerous dimensions.

Easter worship services on April 7 were disrupted in downtown Monrovia, Sinkor, and parts of the Congo Town area. In other parts of the city, churches were jampacked with worshipers celebrating the glorious resurrection of Jesus Christ and invoking the power and presence of God to end this renewed phantasmagoria.

Looting was massive and began with cars. Whoever had a vehicle had it taken away. Companies that imported and sold used cars were broken into and cars were stolen. Garages where cars were being repaired were raided; and because some of these fighters were mechanics, they knew what to do. Other mechanics were held at gunpoint and made to do makeshift repairs to make cars functional. Even cars belonging to the United Nations and other international and local NGO's were not spared. It was a car festival. This also meant that many accidents occurred as those who could not drive ran into objects and into other cars. They drove with such speed that it was risky crossing the road at any given time.

The fighters used these cars to drive into neighborhoods, where they burglarized homes and businesses and carried off the goods. It is believed most of the cars stolen were taken to Gbarnga and later carried across the border into Guinea or to Ivory Coast where they were sold for amounts far below the original cost. The fighters also looted homes, warehouses, and stores. Many of the fighters also moved into people's homes that were left vacant as people fled to safety; others were asked to leave so that their homes could be used as a "military base" or as a "command post."

A good number of homes and other buildings were burned by both sides. Thick black smoke over the city from time to time indicated that structures were being razed by fire. Those structures that were not burned were looted. The most damaged areas included downtown Monrovia, Camp Johnson Road, Haile Selassie Avenue (commonly called Capitol By-Pass), and parts of Sinkor.

Information revealed that the "government troops" or "allied forces" as they were sometimes called, had surrounded the city with the intention of taking it completely. Some persons argued that this offensive was a continuation of "Operation Octopus" of 1992 and that the ultimate plan was to create an atmosphere where Taylor would be declared president and Alhaji Kromah, his new ally, would become vice president.

The obvious target was the Barclay Training Center (BTC) where it was believed Johnson and his men had taken refuge. The BTC itself was only a stone's throw away from the Executive Mansion and was built to protect the first family. It was a solid structure, and given the location where it is, anybody attempting to capture it would find it a fortress. If Taylor and Kromah wanted to be in charge, they would have to control the BTC; for anyone using the Executive Mansion faced constant threats from soldiers in the BTC.

By this time, foreign nationals were being airlifted by the US Embassy and taken to safety either to Freetown, Sierra Leone, or to Dakar, Senegal. Liberians were left to fend for themselves.

One medium of information we relied on was the radio. During the first few days of the battle, all the local stations continued to broadcast as though things were normal, hardly mentioning the conflict. Monrovia had six frequency modulation (FM) stations at the time. They included Eternal Love Winning Africa (ELWA), which also broadcast simultaneously via short wave (SW) that was owned by the Sudan Interior Mission (SIM); the ELCM of the Roman Catholic Church; Radio Monrovia (ELRM), a private station owned by a businessman, Charles Snetter; DC 101 FM of Fred Bass Golokai, another private station; KISS FM of the National Patriotic Front of Liberia; and the government-owned LBS, known as "Power 91." A good number of persons owned short-wave radios and tuned in regularly to hear reports on Liberia from the British Broadcasting Corporation (BBC) and the Voice of America (VOA). The international stations turned out to be more reliable than the local stations.

During the Easter Mass being celebrated by the Roman Catholic Church in Sacred Heart Cathedral by Archbishop Michael Francis and broadcast over ELCM, gunshots were heard on the radio; in a few minutes, the station was off the air. It had been attacked by gunmen and set ablaze. A few days later, Radio Monrovia was looted and destroyed. Fortunately the transmitter was not damaged badly or stolen. Following the cessation of hostilities, the engineers at Radio Monrovia worked to get it back on the air. DC 101 was looted and the transmitter taken, but it too is back on the air. The government station "Power 91" had been off the air a day or two before the crisis and stayed off. Its service is sporadic; efforts are being made by the international community to keep it broadcasting.

The only two stations that remained on the air were KISS FM of the Front and station ELWA. A month later, the area in which ELWA was located came under attack by men of the LPC advancing on the Congo Town residence of Taylor. When the LPC were finally driven back by the "allied forces," the FM and short-wave transmitters of ELWA were believed pirated.

Some members of the State Council and other officials of government took refuge at the ECOMOG military base. The chairman, Wilton Sankawulo, lost control of the situation. Taylor and Kromah became spokesmen for the government. It was understandable since they were leaders of armed factions. Rumor had it that the chairman sought refuge first at ECOMOG base and later at Taylor's compound. Chairman

Sankawulo had become powerless and voiceless. It was no surprise then, when the hostilities ceased, that he was removed for ineffectiveness.

Councilman Oscar Quiah, known for his stance in supporting the welfare of the ordinary citizen had become ill and was flown to Accra, Ghana, for treatment. The word was that he had hypertension and was on the verge of a stroke when he was flown out of the country.

Councilman George Boley left Monrovia less than a week before the war broke out. Two weeks into the battle, the BBC interviewed Boley in Paris, France. Boley made it clear he was not in favor of the move against Johnson. Taylor and Kromah had insisted on the action. When asked as to whether he intended to return to Liberia, he declared that Monrovia was not Liberia and that he would return to Liberia. The implication of the statement as understood by most listeners was that Dr. Boley was probably in Paris to buy arms to mobilize his LPC to fight Taylor and Kromah.

Sure enough, not long after that rumors began that LPC fighters stationed in southeastern Liberia were making their way toward the capital, Monrovia. The attack on the NPFL during the month of May was by the LPC. They were believed to be siding with ULIMO-J since they were all Krahns.

As the assault on the BTC continued for two months almost nonstop, the leaders of ECOWAS and the UN convened a meeting of factional leaders in Accra, Ghana. This coincided with the meeting of ECOWAS's Committee of Nine specifically set up to deal with the Liberian problem and other matters relating to the war in Liberia. Johnson was flown out of Monrovia much to the dismay and disappointment of Taylor and Kromah. Neither one of them attended the meeting, which ended earlier than scheduled.

The leaders of ECOWAS were annoyed at the behavior of the Liberian factional leaders. President Rawlings of Ghana did not mince words when he told them ECOWAS could no longer squander the resources of their various countries when the leaders of Liberia were not showing enough good will and power to end the war. He revealed that a major decision on Liberia would be reached during the ECOWAS summit scheduled for August in Accra. The Liberian leaders seemed to be trying to wear out the patience of ECOWAS leaders so that they would eventually become tired and pull out of Liberia. When this happened then Liberians would be left at the Liberian leaders' mercy.

The NPFL, especially, had been doing all possible to demoralize and weaken the resolve of ECOMOG. From the attack on ECOMOG when they first landed on Liberian soil, the ultimate purpose was to get ECOMOG out of Liberia. If ECOMOG had withdrawn from Liberia, the country would have divided along factional lines and the war would have continued almost endlessly. Not only was the NPFL seeking to weaken ECOMOG, they were also trying to weaken the people of Liberia and bring them to their knees, thus becoming dependent on the factions.

One of the interesting alliances formed during this recent unrest was between Taylor and Kromah. As stated earlier, ULIMO was formed to serve as a force to neutralize the NPFL during the early days of the NPFL's "Operation Octopus" in 1992. Many Mandingoes were killed, according to information received, because they cooperated with the Doe government in searching out hideouts and supporters of the Front in Nimba. Even before the war, Mandingoes, known as an industrious people, were hated for dominating the socio-economic life of Nimba County and for their exclusive lifestyle. The Mandingoes and Krahns felt the brunt of the Front's offensive. Thus, it is understandable as to why they united forces in the organization of ULIMO.

The split in ULIMO came when the Krahns felt that the Mandingoes were trying to dominate and control the organization by usurping the leadership. They also charged that the welfare of the Krahn fighters was made secondary to that of the Mandingo fighters. The ripples of the rift could be felt in Monrovia as the two groups fought each other to gain territory. It was also revealed that other warring groups that came into existence soon patterned their method of operation after the NPFL. The natural resources, especially gold, diamonds, and timber, were exploited and sold without benefit to the people of Liberia.

Even the US ambassador to Liberia, William Milam, in an interview with CNN in mid-1996, revealed that the factions, especially the NPFL, have mineral-rich land at their disposal that fuels their war machines. Additional comment on this shall be made in a later chapter.

During their stay in Liberia, ECOMOG worked with the government of Liberia in maintaining peace and stability. With the coming of the various factions to Monrovia to make up the government, ECOMOG's responsibility in cooperation with the government continued. It was a dilemma for ECOMOG when the "government" attempted to arrest General Roosevelt Johnson. Should it support the government, at least morally, or discourage the action? Inside sources revealed that Taylor had told the field commander, General John Mark Inienger, that he could take Johnson and the barracks in seventy-two hours.

Prior to this declaration of war on Johnson, the government activated discussions on the Status of Forces Agreement (SOFA). These are written guidelines governing and directing the role and responsibility of ECOMOG so that it does not become a permanent occupying force once peace is achieved. The agreement also forces the government of Liberia to respond to and make ECOMOG's work easy. Previous governments such as the IGNU and LNTG I did not focus on the Status of Forces Agreement. Why the previous governments ignored the Status of Forces Agreement, which had benefits for both ECOMOG and the government of Liberia, is anyone's guess. But when LNTG II brought the Status of Forces Agreement to the forefront, many Liberians did not understand that its significance was a normal procedure. Liberia was not the first country to enter this agreement with friendly foreign forces that were helping maintain law and order and would not be the last. The impression most people got from the insistence of the government and the emphasis placed on the discussion was that the NPFL was trying to limit and restrict the movements and role of ECOMOG in protecting Monrovia and in facilitating the peace process for Liberia. Both ECOWAS and the government of Liberia had skilled persons who were discussing the issues to satisfy both sides. SOFA has now been concluded and enacted into law.

The war that erupted in April 1996 was a major blow to the peace process and to the progress made by Liberians who were trying to put their lives together again. Despite the years of pain, anguish, and agony experienced by the people of Liberia, they were still willing to give their detractors a chance to put their ideas to work. A number of international institutions committed themselves to the rehabilitation of the country and its people. The plan was to move from relief to development and to help Liberians become self-sustaining. The hopes that were raised with the coming of the factional leaders were dashed and smashed, throwing the country into a great and bleak depression. Nobody wants to invest resources into a volatile, combustible situation only to lose. Development requires stability, law, order, and infrastructure. The Book of Psalms encourages those who trust in the Lord to remember that "weeping may linger for the night, / but joy comes with the morning." The gladness that came with the morning of the factional leaders' arrival was suddenly turned to sadness, dancing was turned to mourning, and joy was turned into sorrow. The morning is breaking.

THREE

WHO BENEFITS?

EFFORTS to end the war in Liberia came from a number of sources. The UN became involved with efforts of ECOWAS and the OAU. All these attempts seemed to be fruitless. Someone was getting the most out of a bad situation. Who reaped benefits from the deaths of Liberians? Who gained profits from the deaths of Liberians? What did they gain through the prolongation of the war?

The first group to benefit from the war in Liberia is the arms dealers from the West and their cohorts in West Africa and Liberia. While it is true that generally there are no real winners in war as everyone loses in one way or another, these arms dealers reap huge profits from the racket of the arms trade. This trade is conducted openly and on the underground market. Several sources of arms were available to Liberia dissidents.

First, with the dissolution of the Soviet Union and the decline of Communism in Eastern Europe, the large stocks of arms that were in those countries as a deterrent to hostilities and a catalyst of the Cold War were disposed of. Many of those arms and other heavy weapons were made available to Third World countries, Liberia being no exception. The price of these weapons dropped at the end of the Cold War. According to reliable sources it was possible to get an out-dated jet bomber for as little as fifty thousand dollars. One can only imagine the cost of smaller weapons.

The unification of Germany was another source of arms. This union saw the absorption of East Germany. Probably the United Germany, in maintaining a level on par with other Western countries, got rid of the less sophisticated arms of East Germany, which found their way to arms dealers who subsequently traded these to Liberia and other countries.

The third source from which Liberia warring factions probably obtained arms was the US, which is considered the world's leading supplier of arms. Due to the nature of American history and culture, the right to bear arms by ordinary citizens is having far-reaching effects not only in America but on many Third World nations. Purchasing a gun in the US is as simple as going to the supermarket. The Liberians in the US found it easy to contact an arms supplier to get arms to Liberia.

A fourth and major source of arms is France. The Ivory Coast and Burkina Faso, both former French colonies, are neighboring countries of Liberia. The president of Burkina Faso, Blaise Campore, is believed to be married to a relative of Felex Houphouet Boigny, late president of the Ivory Coast. Boigny was believed to be a major supporter of Charles Taylor and the NPFL. Samuel Doe killed President William Tolbert and his son, A. Benedict Tolbert. A.B., as he was affectionately called, was married to the daughter of President Boigny. They had been married less than a year when his father was overthrown and they both were killed. The agony it caused the Boigny family put a strain on Liberian-Ivory Coast relations and created a distance between Presidents Doe and Boigny. This made Boigny throw his full weight behind Taylor and the NPFL in their attempt to overthrow the Doe government. The contacts this gave Taylor in France, especially for arms, cannot be fully comprehended; but it is fair to conclude that the French arms dealers benefited immensely from the Liberian war.

One can imagine how other arms dealers in Europe and Asia benefited from the war in Liberia. While the blood and tears flowed from the people of Liberia, the arms dealers found a partnership with NPFL, ULIMO, LPC, and their partners.

Indeed, the ones who benefited the most from the war in Liberia are the NPFL, ULIMO, LPC, and LDF. In order to pay for the massive arms buildup, these warring factions controlled the natural resources of the nation that they extracted and sold or gave in exchange for arms. As a major beneficiary of the war in Liberia, the warring factions profited from a big business in the trading of the resources of which more will be said later.

The supply of arms was a major factor in the prolongation of the war, and since the Western nations were the major suppliers of arms, it is necessary to appeal to their moral sense of responsibility not to support the sale of arms to rebel groups. Churches and civic organizations in Western nations are called on to pressure their governments on Liberia's behalf so that the war does not flare up again. The effects of the war on this small West African country are devastating. Apart from the destruction of the infrastructure, which many Western nations may help rebuild, the people have been exposed to grave dangers of death and mutilation, torture and other inexpressible horrors. The development of human resources has been hampered, the young people have been denied and deprived of the opportunity of discovering themselves, actualizing their potential, and contributing to the development of Liberia.

The nations of the world belong to a common community usually described as the global village. The large, industrialized nations may think they are so independent of the smaller, developing nations that they feel no obligation to putting an end to war in those countries. But one can invoke the principles of international charters found in the UN, the Geneva Conventions, and others. Furthermore, the destruction of one nation forces its citizens to flee to other nations where the traumatic experience of being uprooted and disconnected from the homeland creates problems for the host country.

In order to stop the recurrence of this flow of blood in Liberia, I am appealing to Western nations to help maintain peace in Liberia. What can they do? They can help stop the importation of arms to Liberia. While most of these nations practice the free enterprise system where private businesses are allowed to function, the international sale of arms should be made illegal. Western countries have the means through sophisticated equipment and well-trained security personnel to halt the flow of arms in and out of their countries. They can make the illegal importation of arms difficult if not impossible.

Not only can Western nations obstruct or hinder the flow of arms, they can also destroy the stockpile of arms they have removed from their active arsenals. The dormant stockpile of weapons, though outdated for a Western nation, can still cause death and destruction and are therefore still dangerous. If Western nations fail to assist developing nations in restricting the arms trade, how can they ensure that these same arms will not find their way back to their own countries in terrorists' hands? Though Liberians have never been involved in terrorist acts in other countries, a network of arms dealers could be formed; and established governments could have serious problems. Evidence seems to suggest that the NPFL fighters trained in Libya were planning to destabilize West Africa. They were believed to be responsible for the war in Sierra Leone and the disorder of Senegal and Gambia. It is expedient and appropriate that the arms race to Liberia and other Third World countries be checked. Rumors in Monrovia even pointed to the Zairean conflict as an offshoot of the Liberian war, as it was reported in local papers that former fighters were being recruited for Zaire. Most of those accused have since denied it.

While Liberians were dying and languishing in refugee camps, unscrupulous people were benefiting from the war. The first beneficiaries we have recognized are the arms dealers. We have identified likely countries that reaped the most benefits from Liberia's war through the sale of arms from dealers in those countries. We appealed to Western countries to help in obstructing the flow of arms to Liberia and recommended possible ways to assist in this process.

However, the arms dealers are not the only beneficiaries in the Liberian war. A second group of beneficiaries includes some West African countries.

We must not underestimate or minimize the role and contribution of the leaders of West Africa, especially in organizing ECOMOG. The financial, moral, and humanitarian support given to Liberia kept the nation from being totally destroyed, even to the point of creating economic and social problems in some ECOWAS nations. ECOMOG supported the Liberian government against the rebels until rebels became a part of the government, thus putting ECOMOG in a difficult position as the April 1996 blunder showed. History will judge the West African initiative as a timely, worthwhile venture that is being emulated elsewhere. However, there are always deviants in all well-meaning organizations, and ECOMOG and ECOWAS are not free from those who would spoil and tarnish the good names of these organizations.

The country of ECOWAS that has benefited the most from Liberia's war is the Ivory Coast. At the start of the war, the Ivorian town of Danane, where I lived in exile, was a village without running water, with barely any electricity, and with only one paved road. Today, Danane has grown into a modern city with all the facilities that make life convenient.

Before Gbarnga became the headquarters of the NPFL, Taylor and the top brass of the Front lived in Danane. In order to establish his presence in Danane, it is believed Taylor contributed immensely to the development of Danane. He had no choice. If this was to be his base, he had to spend money to give it a facelift and to ensure security for himself.

The money Taylor used may have been taken from the resources of Liberia. Looting was a favorite method of operation of his men and the majority of goods looted from Liberia ended up in the Ivory Coast. It is said that when the NPFL transported weapons and ammunition to Liberia, the area where the convoy was to pass was blacked out. We can fairly conclude that these acts of accommodation did not go unrewarded.

In addition to the role of Taylor in helping to develop parts of the Ivory Coast, the Liberian refugees themselves played significant roles in the socioeconomic development of many Ivorian towns. The Ivory Coast never declared Liberians as refugees and consequently never established refugee camps as was the case in several other West African nations. Refugees in the Ivory Coast were considered as tourists and guests and were treated as such. When they rented rooms or homes they were required to pay far beyond the worth of the house or room. They were also made to pay all kinds of fees; and whenever relatives of Liberians (particularly in the US) sent them money, they were forced to spend all of it. This did not only take place in Danane, it was true also in Tabou, Man, San Pedro, and other towns in the Ivory Coast.

The Ivory Coast, as a member of ECOWAS, never sent troops to join ECOMOG; and during the last years was among the least active in ECOWAS, though it benefited most. The Ivory Coast's lack of support was glaring and there was little anyone could do. Attempts to get the Ivorian leadership to desist from this passive attitude came from international organizations. The United States made direct appeals and even threats, but all fell on deaf ears in the Ivory Coast.

Some Liberians in the US went as far as warning the Ivory Coast that just as they continued to destabilize Liberia, it was possible for that to be done in their country; but nothing slowed down that country's support for the NPFL and the flow of arms through it. Only when President Boigny died did any meaningful change become evident in Taylor's willingness to cooperate. Only in 1995 did the Ivory Coast send an envoy to Liberia and agree to send some medical personnel to serve with ECOMOG in Liberia.

In reality, Taylor was probably aware that the death of Boigny would force a foreign policy change in the Ivory Coast. Therefore he changed his strategy from being an outsider to being an insider, thus hiding behind the camouflage of a government and being able to legitimize his actions in relationship with the Ivory Coast.

In addition to the antagonism of Boigny for Doe, Boigny played the Anglophone/Francophone game to Liberia's disadvantage. One of the elements that hinder African unity is the legacy of colonialism; one part of that legacy is language: French and English. Though independent now, the ties to the former colonial rulers are stronger than ties to other African nations, with Francophone nations enjoying a solidarity not shared with Anglophone nations.

Though Senegal and Guinea, two Francophone nations, sent troops, Guinea did so, not only to help bring peace to Liberia, but mainly to protect itself from the war in Liberia, because Guinea is one of Liberia's immediate neighbors. Senegal's stay in Liberia was short-lived but significant because these troops helped defeat "Operation Octopus." Whether it was true that Senegal went to Liberia under pressure from the US, their withdrawal showed the difficulties ECOMOG/ECOWAS had to work with. Greater progress on Liberia is made when an Anglophone head of state chairs ECOWAS than when a Francophone leader does.

Another West African nation that benefited as much as, if not more than the Ivory Coast is Guinea. Before the inception of the war in Liberia, a modern system of transportation in the border towns of N'zerekore and surrounding villages was nonexistent. Today, a large fleet of taxis and other vehicles are plying the streets and roads of the Forest Region of Guinea. Suffice it to say also that, like the border towns in the Ivory Coast, the frontier towns in Guinea have been developed during the past six years. Diecke, a small village with less than two thousand population before the war in Liberia is now a medium-size town with over five thousand people. Needless to say, other facilities also are owned by Liberian refugees and other nationals who fled the war in Liberia.

Other West African countries where Liberians went as refugees also benefited, but not as much as the Ivory Coast and Guinea. In Ghana, Benin, Togo, Senegal, and Nigeria, Liberians were supported to a large extent by friends and relatives in the United States and Europe. In some of those places, such as Ghana, Liberians were not permitted to work; thus they had to establish small businesses in the refugee camps. The purchasing power of Liberian refugees in West Africa was of concern in some quarters, and they have been recognized as a unique set of refugees. In fact, a Ghanaian banker is quoted as saying that during his several years of banking experience in Ghana, the US dollars have never gone through their banking system as they have been since the arrival of Liberian refugees in Ghana.

This is not to say Liberians were not problematic. Some became involved in counterfeiting, drugs, thievery, the sale of arms, and other social vices. The loud-mouth, argumentative, and arrogant tendencies of many Liberians caused their hosts to refuse to allow them to live in some areas. On the whole, Liberians were as much liabilities as they were assets.

Who benefits from the Liberian war while the Liberians themselves are suffering, dying, and in exile? Arms dealers benefit. Some African countries and people benefit. Thirdly, some ECOMOG soldiers benefit. True, many ECOMOG soldiers have given their lives for peace in Liberia. Some have been killed, some have been maimed, and some have been physically disabled.

While most of the ECOMOG soldiers are professional soldiers, well trained and disciplined, other soldiers' primary purpose for going to Liberia is different from peacekeeping. Liberia is a small country; and Monrovia, where ECOMOG was concentrated, could hardly keep a secret. Some of our ECOMOG friends have shared that some countries developed a practice of sending their problem soldiers to Liberia as soon as they started causing trouble. By sending them to Liberia, these leaders thought they were getting rid of their problem soldiers.

Unfortunately, active service in ECOMOG made some of those soldiers more troublesome. The presence of these soldier helps explain why the coup in Gambia and Sierra Leone and the military unrest in Guinea were mostly engineered by former ECOMOG soldiers.

Some soldiers have made peacekeeping a business. They sell weapons to warring factions and become involved in illegal trade. They ship home cars and electrical appliances that were bought for very little or received as compensation for military assistance. In more ways than one, ECOMOG soldiers themselves are beneficiaries of the Liberian war. Some have become so comfortable living in Liberia that they return as businessmen and women after their discharge from their home army. Some played the factions against one another and benefited immensely.

While I can identify external beneficiaries of the war in Liberia, those who really benefited the most are the warring factions. At the onset of the conflict, they made promises they could not keep. Taylor and the NPFL were known for breaking agreements and giving flimsy reasons. More than ten conferences have been held on Liberia. Sometimes at these conferences Taylor has taken time to build up his arms supply. All the time the warring factions have benefited immensely by continuing to sell the mineral resources of Liberia while the unarmed civilians are losing everything. The warring factions have arms, can escape danger, and are trained to kill and to survive.

This means that as long as the war continued, the civilians were at the mercy of these bandits who marginalized, maimed, destroyed, disgraced, and killed them. Many respectable individuals have been brought from a place of decency to a place of disgrace. As the war dragged on, the warring factions became richer and richer, more and more powerful, while those without arms became poorer and poorer, losing their sense of what it means to be human and Liberian.

Whenever a skirmish or outbreak of war occurred, the civilians were asked and usually forced to leave their homes, thus becoming uprooted from homes and villages. Their family covenant was destroyed as they were torn apart, becoming people without a town, village, and property, even people without a sense of culture and belonging.

The warring factions in Liberia were not paid regularly by their leaders and therefore tended to use the war to pay themselves by looting and vandalizing. The NPFL was so large that Taylor did not know how many men made up the NPFL. The same is true about LPC, LDF, and ULIMO. Whenever there was an outbreak of fighting, homes were looted and properties were stolen. What people worked for and accumulated over the years was taken in a matter of minutes or hours.

Liberia has experienced three outbreaks of war. The years 1990, 1992, and 1996 marked armed offensives against the people of Liberia by the NPFL. The notorious 1992 "Operation Octopus" was decisively put down by ECOMOG. Between 1992 and 1995, the people of Monrovia and its surrounding areas made conscious efforts to rebuild their lives. We believe some level of sense and sensibility was returning to the Monrovia area. Businesses and jobs were returning; and though things were tough, Liberians were determined to move forward with their lives. In the absence of electricity and water, the residents had adjusted to a lower-than-normal lifestyle and were doing fine under the circumstances.

The April catastrophe started by the "government" threw the city and its environs into a difficult downhill ride that will take years to reverse. The level of looting that took place in Monrovia reduced the structures to bare "skeletons" or worse. Anybody thinking of doing any serious investing in Liberia during the seven dark years has to think twice and carefully. As long as the rebels made up the government, they were irresponsible and dangerous, unreliable when it came to keeping their word on anything.

The senior citizens suffered the worst fate of all. They were hoping to see a glimmer of peace before passing on; but many of them were never able to rebuild or renovate their homes and lives that were damaged by the civil war. The middle-aged can continue to hope for better, but they cannot expect to rebuild their lives soon. One of the interesting things about Liberians is that, in order to survive, a good number of them took sides and joined a faction through which they obtained jobs. Many of them did not serve in active combat, but they are guilty by association of all the crimes committed by these factions.

The young adults, youth, and children were in the most precarious plight. They had time in their favor; but with the destruction of schools and the decline of the educational system, it was difficult for them to get any serious education. Those who owned and operated schools in Monrovia were hesitant about reopening; however, church-related schools continue unabated despite the tribulations endured to provide quality education. Huge amounts of money were spent to renovate and reactivate the schools that were damaged in 1990, 1992, and 1996. A large portion of funds for educational and other institutions, especially those that were private and church-operated, came from overseas. The Partners in Mission spent money from resources, and because of stewardship responsibilities they have to be more careful. The young people faced a dilemma. If they stayed in Monrovia, the chances of getting a decent education were slim. But by leaving Liberia, they were uncertain of sponsorship. Many young people who are living in exile and in Liberia have not been in school for the last seven years.

The next generation of Liberian leaders must seek to be different and pursue progress and development. The concern of our leaders must be the future of the nation. We must seek national interest and make Liberia a stable country. Because of the April 6, 1996, disaster, thousands of other Liberians became refugees. In May 1996, three ships carrying Liberians from the war zone in Monrovia made international news when several West African nations refused them entry. Fortunately two of the ships, the *Bulk Challenge* and the *Victory Reefer,* were allowed to dock in Ghana and Sierra Leone respectively. The third ship was not allowed to dock in any West African port and had to return to Monrovia, the city of death.

The life civilians were forced to lead made one wonder as to whether the life of a slave is not better than that of a refugee. The slave has an owner who, because of his own benefit, will take care of the slave, provide food, shelter, and health benefits. The refugee is at the mercy of the host country and has no home and no one to care for him or her. The refugee is usually intimidated and harassed by security agents of the host country. Fortunately, the international charters provide the conditions for the care of the refugees and allow them to maintain their freedom and basic human rights.

During the seven years of darkness in Liberia, the warring factions were the leading beneficiaries of the war. Living on the blood, sweat, and tears of the ordinary Liberian people, not only did these factions benefit from the natural resources of the country, they became obsessive about their own security. Taylor had the highest number of bodyguards. When he traveled from his home in Congo Town about five miles from the Executive Mansion where he worked until a shoot-out at the mansion on October 31, 1996, his convoy included about seven vehicles of security personnel, two eighteen-seater buses, one ECOMOG jeep, and five assorted cars, not counting the cars he personally included. An insider revealed that a large amount of arms was hidden in the buses to be used in case of an attack. It is interesting to note that those who threaten the lives of others are most afraid of death. Later, the number of cars decreased but not substantially.

The faction leaders enjoyed many benefits that deprived the civilians of several opportunities. They rode in plush cars, lived in fancy homes, and traveled extensively with large entourages; but the ordinary Liberian could not even afford to buy a used car or, worse, did not have the five Liberian dollars to take a taxi to the city center. Taxi fare increased after the April 6 disaster. The displaced centers are crowded with Liberians who owned their homes or could afford rent and managed farms. The constant fighting has reduced them to the level of beggars.

I reside in Congo Town. Before Councilmen Taylor and Kromah moved in, it was a calm, peaceful, and lively place where boys and girls from miles around came to visit, play football and kickball, and interact with one another. It was a community where, because of the shortage of water, particularly during the months of December to May each year, residents of the area went to fetch water from the well that was constructed by the United Methodist Committee on Relief (UMCOR). Today, the area is so militarized that where Taylor lives is known as "Charlesville" and has a reputation for being dangerous. I live near Kromah and a large gate has been constructed to the entrance of my place so that the area has become out of bounds to visitors and residents alike. In short, the arrival of the warring factions as members of the government has brought no significant development and no improved standard of living for the people.

Not the least beneficiaries of the Liberian war were those

Liberians and international personnel working for the United Nations and other well-paying NGO's. Each time the war flares up and subsides, relief and other organizations spring up in numbers to help ease the burdens of the war. Many of these jobs and contracts pay so well that those who have them do not want the war to end as it might mean an end to their jobs. They make enough hard currency that, when changed on the Liberian-paralleled market, their earnings are equivalent to a thousand times more than what the ordinary Liberian makes. These Liberians do not seem to have considered the possibility that, when peace comes, they will make the same or even better.

Some UN personnel are international and think on the same level as these Liberians. Some of the international employees come from some of the poorer nations of the world. Many of them make as much as five hundred United States dollars ($500.00) a day. They live so fabulously above the ordinary Liberian that some of them create social problems and live as kings and queens.

It is unfair that so many people in Liberia suffer unjustly while a comparatively few reap enormous benefits from Liberia. Arms dealers in some West African countries benefit from the suffering of Liberians. Those who really became rich off the deaths of Liberians were the warring factions and their leaders. Then there are the ordinary Liberians and international personnel working for the United Nations and other international NGO's who think that as long as the war lasts, there will be money in their pockets to, as Liberians put it, "make their pots boil."

The international community must not ignore and neglect Liberia. The country has the potential of being a greater and stronger nation than it was before. As Liberia suffers, the world suffers. As a signatory to major charters around the world, Liberia's status commands and deserves serious attention for Liberia's development and progress to be facilitated. There are enough trained, professional personnel in Liberia who can lead their country to a better future. Those who must benefit most from Liberia must be Liberians themselves.

FOUR

WHAT'S THE DIFFERENCE?

EORGE Orwell's classic political allegory *Animal Farm* is the story of a revolution that changed face, but in practice remained the same or was worse at some points. Liberia has had two revolutions: The 1980 revolution supposedly "In the Cause of the People," and the 1990 revolution led by Charles Taylor and the National Patriotic Front of Liberia (NPFL). This chapter examines the two revolutions, particularly the latter one, and discourages future attempts to change the course of the nation by force.

Usually, when people advocate sociopolitical change, they produce a manifesto, a political platform or program of reform that leads to progress and serves as a blueprint to where they want to lead the nation. The revolutions in Liberia produced no such plan and seemed to be for the sake of revolution. No marked change was produced that led to progress and development.

The architects of the first revolution claim they introduced a multi-party system into Liberia. That seems to be a "feather in their caps." When one considers the level of violence, bloodshed, and destruction that followed, it makes one wonder if they had followed a plan of social change what would have happened?

During the 1980 revolution, promises of improved life and better conditions had people dancing in the streets. Within less than three years, tyranny showed its ugly head and dictatorship became the hallmark of the Doe regime. A book by Professor Paul Gifford, *Christianity and Politics in Doe's Liberia*, portrayed the Doe government as so brutal, repressive, and suppressive that almost every pressure group and critical institution or association was neutralized. Though Gifford does not recognize it, the church remained the only moral authority during the decade of the Doe regime in Liberia. The 1980 revolution was a disappointment. It became obvious early on that Doe intended to prolong his stay in power; any opposition was targeted and crushed. Doe was worse than Tolbert whom he criticized as corrupt and oppressive. The change for the better that was expected did not come; instead Doe did everything he accused Tolbert of with greater intensity.

At the start of the 1980 revolution, civil servants' salaries were increased by almost 200 percent. That increase was a welcome relief from the low income many Liberians had been receiving. At that time, the United States dollar was legal tender in Liberia, and so the standard of living of Liberians was expected to rise. But Doe overturned his own good deeds and intentions by abolishing the hut tax and the head tax, which boosted the revenue from Liberian's rural regions and were used to develop those areas. Doe also began deducting 25 percent of the civil servants' income. The joke was circulated that he meant to say twenty-five *dollars*, thus revealing the low level of expense and education he had and the poor advice he received. Doe also introduced some strenuous new taxes and a new Liberian currency. This new currency was supposed to be on par with the US dollar, but the reality was otherwise as the Liberian dollar went from a rate of one US dollar to two Liberian dollars to an average rate of fifty Liberian dollars to one US dollar.

The brutal nature of the Doe government made many Liberians, irrespective of tribe or ethnic background, identify with Taylor and the NPFL. Nobody wanted another ten years under Doe. This desire for a new government made many see the NPFL as a breath of fresh air and not the suffocating wind it became. The initial successes of the NPFL were partly due to the cooperative nature and willing contributions of the Liberian people both at home and abroad.

At the beginning of the 1990 war, Taylor declared to the Liberian people that he was launching a popular revolution not for power for himself but to free the Liberian people from the grips of Doe's death machine. Taylor claimed he wanted to give Liberians a chance to live better lives where everyone could go to bed without fear and intimidation; he promised freedom, justice, and peace.

Taylor further accused Doe of destroying the economy, repressing the people, becoming an autocrat, and having no respect for the constitution. These words would indict Taylor himself later on. Taylor and his NPFL became guilty of the "animal farm syndrome," which is the tendency of returning to corrupt practices and a greed for power. There were few differences between the results of his revolution and the revolution of Doe.

The soldiers of the Front were described as "Freedom Fighters" even though they took away the freedom of the people. Under the NPFL rule, people had little or no rights. In areas where the NPFL presence was felt, lives were constantly threatened and given less worth; liberties were snatched; rights suspended; and only those connected with the NPFL in some way or another enjoyed any level of freedom and happiness.

When the pressure groups such as ULIMO and LPC came to force the Front to end the war against Liberians, they all ended up dancing to the beat of the same drum. They, too, exploited the country's natural resources and became rich enough to buy more arms and keep the war going. At peace conferences on Liberia, they bargained for positions that would keep them in power. They have failed the hopes of the Liberian people, and Liberians generally agree that they were all the same and that there was no difference in their behavior.

The economic strain of supporting a five- or six-person presidency was stressful and burdensome on the Liberian people. Each person had a full-time staff to cater to his or her needs and demanded more than she or he was entitled to. They constantly bickered and argued over trivial matters while the ordinary citizens of Liberia suffered. There was a time when civil servants' salaries were delayed up to a year as the ministry of finance, the National Bank of Liberia, and the Council of State had a war of words over who was responsible.

LNTG II seemed inefficient and irresponsible, and anybody criticizing it was targeted for brutal treatment. No recognizable or significant development occurred while both LNTG's were in power. Both being factional governments, they tended to reward their fighters and sympathizers with jobs.

The major source of income for the government of Liberia for most of the seven years was the Maritime Fund. Due to the number of ships registered under the Liberian flag, described as the "flag of convenience," the nation was told that the government received two million US dollars a month. So it was a real shock when a disgruntled legislator of ULIMO-K disclosed that the government received twenty-one million dollars and not two as previously reported. He was subsequently thrown out of the legislature because all the legislators were either appointed by a factional head or "elected" by a few supposed representatives from the counties and districts; in reality they were still factional appointees.

Interestingly, Liberia had a wealth of well-trained professionals and technocrats still in the country, although the "brain drain" from the war could be felt. However, many of these technocrats were "bought" by the system and became lax in their commitment. Many of them joined the leaders who lived luxuriously. A good number of these Liberian professionals studied on the graduate and post-graduate level in the United States and in Europe. Having traveled abroad and after seeing what progress and development is, they might be expected to transfer these methods and policies for the benefit of the nation. Instead, these technocrats and professionals allowed themselves to be ruled by materialism and their leadership style dictated by greed, making themselves what Liberians call "gravy-seekers."

Doe had only a high school education, but he gathered around himself a corps of well-educated men and women. Rather than helping to chart a positive course of direction for the nation, they became greedy, grabbing whatever they could get. A culture of lies, deception, and misinformation was developed; and Doe became a monster afraid of his own shadow, believing these pathetic liars and trusting no one, even those who meant well. They ended up destroying him.

Dr. Amos Sawyer was one of the most educated leaders Liberia has had in a long time. During his tenure as interim president, he gathered around himself the "cream of the crop" of Liberian professionals and intellectuals. They had the opportunity to decisively defeat the NPFL and even capture Taylor during the infamous "Operation Octopus," but this probably would have meant the absence of chances to become rich quick without being accountable. As a result, the Interim Government of National Unity (IGNU), sometimes referred to by Taylor as the "Imported Government of No Use," became inefficient. Only during his last days did Sawyer advocate the disarmament policy that some thought was a ploy to keep himself in power. IGNU failed to move forward significantly. It was only able to establish a basic atmosphere of survival.

Presently, the war has taken Liberia back more than a hundred years. The feeder roads that lead to the markets from the farms have become so poor and unmaintained that they have become footpaths. School buildings have declined and no new schools have been built. The United Nations and other international NGO's have literally run the health sector of the country, keeping epidemics at bay.

Liberia was saturated with arms, and a sizable portion of the youth population fought in the war. Guns gave these young people security and a sense of self-esteem, but the government humanitarian organizations can institute a number of measures that will motivate and stimulate the young people and deter them from returning to the armed struggle.

Our leaders must seek to make a difference as they plan to move Liberia into the twenty-first century. Problems need to be tackled from a number of angles. Catching up with the information age and the world of technology is one priority; but we ought to remember that many of the villages in Liberia were burned, and farms have not been worked on for seven years in some areas. The young men and women that once held arms should be given some immediate basic skills that will enable them to return to their villages and towns and to help rebuild them. By giving farmers tools as they return to the land, agriculture will take an important place in the lives of the people.

The development of Liberia is not the sole responsibility of the government. The support and encouragement of Liberian local and grassroots initiatives are suggested. It is expected that civic education, business education, health education, family education, community welfare education, among others, will dominate the drive toward self-sustainability.

One lesson we ought to learn from the war if we wish to make a difference is that no group of Liberians should seek to dominate the rest of Liberians. Equally so, no one group should be marginalized or targeted for annihilation. Liberians may not agree on every point of how to move the country forward; but it is important that respect, acceptance, courtesy, and other characteristics mark our co-existence. We must find richness in diversity. The tendency of treating opposition as enemies and antagonists should be stopped.

Industrialized nations like France and others should be ashamed of letting themselves be used by Taylor, Borley, Johnson, the Ivory Coast, and Burkina Faso. Is France not rich enough that it has to stoop to immoral behavior for a few extra dollars? And if they want to enjoy the resources of Liberia, can they not buy them from a legitimate government?

The churches in these industrialized nations are called upon to exert pressure on their governments to take active steps to discourage illegal action on the part of their governments. It is their Christian duty to help avoid future wars in Africa and Liberia. It does not make sense for them to bandage wounds in the form of relief when they can help to stop the bullets that cause the wounds. The funds used toward relief in Liberia can go a long way in developing an active, unbiased, and progressive country. As a founding member of the UN, the OAU, ECOWAS, and a member of the world community that has contributed to the development of the world, Liberia must claim the attention of the world. It is a moral obligation.

FIVE

THE PROBLEMS WITHIN

LIBERIA suffered from internal and external problems. While some outside forces were responsible for and contributed to the war in Liberia, internal problems were ultimately responsible for the anarchy that descended upon the nation in 1990.

As we discuss these problems, we will first of all review the two major public policies that were supposed to provide the basis for development and stability. Secondly, the three institutions that determine the growth, productivity, and security of the nation will be considered. Thirdly, the chapter will close with reflection on the political, economic, legal, and social systems and where they fell short of providing order and justice.

There is a tendency among the Liberians to blame many of the present socioeconomic and political problems of their country on William V. S. Tubman, Sr., eighteenth president of Liberia. Can the Tubman era be taken in isolation? What role did the previous seventeen presidents before Tubman play in preparing the Liberia that Tubman inherited? Can the institution of slavery as practiced in North America be recognized as a contributing factor to Liberia's problems?

Tubman ascended to the Liberian presidency in 1944 when World War II was still raging and colonialism by the major nations of Europe, many of whom were at war, was entrenched in Africa. A little over a decade later, the wind of political liberation would sweep the continent, and African nations would become independent one after another.

Tubman relied heavily on his technocrats to make the necessary plans and programs of the government operational. Unfortunately, in many cases, most of these technocrats were more interested in their personal gain than in the interests of the nation. Tubman trusted their judgment and gave the necessary cooperation only to realize later that many project proposals that were presented for approval and funding did not exist or were not as elaborate as they seemed. As a result of this negative tendency, the millions of dollars that came into Liberia as revenue, loans, or grants for development ended up in personal pockets and bank accounts.

Being a Pan-Africanist, Tubman spent more time addressing the problems associated with the liberation struggle of the continent than with Liberia's development. Liberia was a founding member and original signatory to the charters of the United Nations (UN), the Organization of African Unity (OAU), the International Court of Justice (ICJ), the International Labor Organization (ILO), the Economic Community of West African States (ECOWAS), and the Mano River Union (MRU) uniting Liberia, Guinea, and Sierra Leone. It is fair to say that Liberia under Tubman's reign had clearer foreign policies than national policies, and this may have contributed to the neglect of the nation. In reality, Tubman's era of rule in Liberia was probably in a more advantageous position to move Liberia further. Therefore he is blamed for not doing enough to develop the nation. The causes of the war in Liberia will be viewed from Tubman's administration.

Development and stability were to be provided by two public policies that characterized Tubman's twenty-seven-year-rule. The first was the "Open Door Policy" and the second was the "Unification Policy." The "Open Door" was meant to attract investment and provide a safe haven for those involved in the political struggle for independence. It was also meant for Liberia to become a home for all people of Negro descent seeking freedom from oppression and suppression anywhere in the world.

Investment did come. However, lax and loosely written contracts and agreements led to the loss of much-needed revenue and industry. Many corporations operated in Liberia under substandard conditions and shady principles. The rubber, mining, agriculture, and shipping industries, which should have made Liberia a developed nation, were allowed to set their own standards in Liberia.

Slavery had existed in North America for more than one hundred fifty years, spanning five generations. Though the slaves were taken from West Africa, they were stripped of their culture, their identity, and their humanity. The slaves were further made to feel inferior to the masters and were brainwashed to believe the culture that they originally possessed was paganistic and heathenistic. With such indoctrination, is it not likely that the slaves returned to Africa with an air of superiority over the culture they once belonged to? In addition, is it not possible that the feeling of being sold into slavery by one's own kin may have contributed to the attitude of these former African slaves toward those Africans they met?

One element of Liberian history that has not been emphasized enough is the fact that both major groups, the "Congo" and the "country people" are all settlers. The "Congo" people settled in this area after the liberation from slavery. The "country" people settled in this part of the world from the Sudanic region somewhere in the heart of Africa. This forced migration occurred due to the advance of Islam from the north; this population shift not only took place because of Islam but also because of epidemics, wars, and famines that made people search for a new home. If we can realize that the "love of liberty" is found in every Liberian home, whether liberty from slavery or religious aggression or diseases, we will have no need to become antagonistic toward anyone else.

The Unification Policy was intended to integrate and bridge the gap between the two major groups in Liberia; but more importantly, the Unification Policy was designed to create a Liberia where there would be equal humanity and equal opportunity for all persons.

If there is anything the war teaches about unification, it is obvious it did not take sufficient root to avert the catastrophe. There is a need to emphasize those uniting factors and strengthen Liberia as a nation. If a nation is a group of people that share certain commonalities such as language, religion, socieconomic links, political system, and other pertinent traditions, Liberia needs to forge a nation.

Policies that were designed to strengthen the fabric of our society were misinterpreted, misunderstood, and misrepresented thus rendering Liberia helpless to withstand the storms that raged in its body politic.

Not only were policies made nonfunctional, but the institutions that influence the nature of growth and level of productivity and security were rendered impractical. These institutions were health, education, and military.

Probably the most successful institution in Liberia was the health sector. Each county had a major hospital, well-equipped and fully staffed; almost all these health centers were government owned and operated. In addition, there were five schools of nursing, namely the Tubman National Institute of Medical Arts (TNIMA) run by the government, the Phebe Nursing School owned by the Lutheran Church, the Nursing School of Cuttington University College of the Episcopal Church, the Winifred Harley Nursing School of the United Methodist Church, and the Currans Nursing School also of the Lutheran Church. The A. M. Dogliotti College of Medicine at one time was considered one of the best medical colleges in West Africa. It trained doctors from all over West Africa and beyond. The health institutions in Liberia provided primary health care and made available high standard facilities. Whenever an outbreak of a disease was suspected, the health workers were alert and prompt in arresting the situation and bringing it under control.

The infant mortality rate was reduced and the emergency programs of immunization were increased thus enabling mothers and children to be vaccinated. Diseases that normally plagued developing and underdeveloped countries did not become epidemics in Liberia. If there were unusual situations, personal hygiene was responsible.

Unfortunately, the average life span for the ordinary person did not improve and remained at fifty-five to sixty years. This can be attributed to other factors such as personal lifestyle, the socioeconomic life of the nation, or the political atmosphere. The common problems that troubled the adult Liberian male included heart attacks, high blood pressure, prostate cancer, strokes, and other lifestyle-related problems. For the Liberian adult female, mortality from all forms of cancer is a major concern.

The health care delivery institution in Liberia was above average, but the educational institution was not so fortunate. After almost 150 years of existence as an independent nation, why was there only one university in Liberia? In many of the former colonies of Great Britain, 40 percent of their annual budget goes toward education; but in Liberia, the opposite is true. Education in Liberia received less attention, and 40 percent of the annual budget went toward security and the purchase of arms. The Tubman and Tolbert eras may not have spent this amount on arms, but Tubman especially was so overly concerned about security that Liberia almost became a police state where anyone who differed with the policies of government was suspected of harboring ill feelings and could be placed under surveillance.

The University of Liberia should have had several campuses spread throughout the country with one in the southeast, another in the north and one in the northwest. The refusal of the government to meet the educational needs of the nation, especially of the rural areas, forced the youth population to migrate to Monrovia where they hoped to pursue further education, only to realize the University of Liberia could accommodate only a limited number of students.

The Episcopal Church of Liberia operated the Cuttington University College, a small, private university college. Cuttington was expensive and the average Liberian could not meet the financial requirement. As a result, many high school graduates were disappointed because they could not pursue higher education.

The Tubman College of Technology in Harper, near Monrovia,

is a recent addition, constructed in 1970 as a project of Tubman's seventy-fifth birth celebration in Maryland County. (The legislature passed a law that Tubman's birthday be celebrated each year by a county to bring development to that county.) But the technical college was not opened until 1978.

On the lower level, the government made several positive attempts but could not maintain these schools. Tubman High School in Monrovia was, at one time, one of the best in West Africa; but the government's inability to maintain it caused its decline. Multilateral high schools were opened in two areas of Liberia, and they were meant to provide academic education and vocational training. These schools, in addition to the reputable Booker Washington Institute (BWI), made serious efforts to provide quality education. The teacher training centers also made worthwhile strides toward quality education.

Despite these commendable attempts to maintain a sound educational system, the illiteracy rate remained high because the educational sector did not grow and develop in proportion to Liberia's population. The rural areas were neglected in terms of education, consequently illiteracy was high in those areas. During the war in Liberia, many of the combatants could not read or write and a good number had never been beyond their villages.

If the churches and other private entities had not buttressed the government's educational system, the conditions in Liberia would have been worse. The schools operated by the churches are the best in Liberia, and no matter where they are located in the country, they maintain above-average standards.

Liberia's major educational problem is the absence of post-secondary institutions. There are commercial schools, but these schools tend only to upgrade the high school education and provide some basic skills that should have been obtained in high school. Liberia has a dire need for colleges and universities. As a matter of fact, the entire educational system of Liberia needs to be reviewed and restructured. While the liberal academic education has its merits, it is necessary for it to be supported by vocational institutions either to be added to these already existing academic institutions or to be made separate entities.

The neglect of its citizens' education, especially in the rural areas is a major factor in the continuation of this war. The lack of education meant underemployment and therefore below-standard lifestyles. Knowing their chances of acquiring the desired education for a decent job was slim, many young men and women have found solace and meaning in bearing arms. Through their weapons they have acquired wealth and property they would not obtain otherwise.

The third institution that this writer intends to consider is the military. Providing security and protection are the primary functions of the military. For a long time Liberia did not have a standing army; the Frontier Force existed to maintain Liberia's borders that were being encroached upon by the French and British governments seeking to expand their colonies in West Africa.

One of the most serious errors made by the Liberian government, especially during the Tubman regime, was the nature of the army. When the government decided it needed a standing army, it tended to enlist mainly indigenous males who were generally illiterate or poorly educated. The army received substandard military and academic training. Liberia had no standing college or institution of higher learning for the training of the military. Army personnel were trained to be brutal, and many of the soldiers were used as watchmen or private bodyguards of government officials. While the Liberian army did serve in the Congo as part of peacekeeping efforts during the crises there, the role of the army in Liberia was vague. The United States, from time to time, offered short-term training to a small number of officers selected by the Liberian government and sent to the United States.

On the whole, the military in Liberia was overlooked, underpaid, neglected, and underestimated. The discontent and confusion among the army was probably intensified when in 1979, during the rice riots, Tolbert, who was president at the time, called on the Guinean government to send troops to Monrovia to quiet the disturbance. It was evident at that time that the army, being dissatisfied with this move on the part of the government, could be bought for a dime. No wonder the military came to power one year later.

During the ten years of rule by the military, it became obvious that the military was poorly educated and could not relate properly to civilians. The brutality of the military during this era is cause for concern. The National Patriotic Front of Liberia (NPFL), itself an army though a rebel army, insisted it came in response to the brutality of the Doe military-supported government. But the NPFL was no less than what the military under Doe was. The army in Liberia needs to be restructured and retrained. The soldiers need training in disaster rescue operations, emergency response, civics, including the constitution, civilian life, and some liberal arts.

With educational and military institutions falling short and health attempting to maintain some balance, one can see how problems could become compounded. Though there were attempts to produce a healthy society, without a sound educational program and a below-standard military, there were bound to be problems. These were some of the internal problems Liberia had that finally erupted into a full-scale war.

We need also to reflect on the political, legal, and socioeconomic systems and how they contributed to the war. Liberia's political system is described as a democratic system, but it has been more of a patronage system than anything else. This attitude may have been cultivated from the traditional chieftancy system where the chief, though supported by a council of elders, remained the sole authority. In any case, a personality cult developed around the president and he, especially Tubman, was made the "law and gospel" of Liberia.

In an attempt to maintain himself in power, Tubman introduced a system in which individuals in the counties received an amount of $66.66 monthly for doing virtually nothing. It not only created an atmosphere of laziness it also facilitated an environment of mistrust and suspicion as those receiving the grant felt obligated to please the president and doing it through scapegoating and witch hunting.

Tubman intimidated his political opponents by threats, coercion, and manipulation. He eventually forged a one-party state that became problematic. The one-party state undermined the unification policy by excluding the majority of the indigenous of Liberia from active politics.

Elections were a farce. The caucus system superseded the will of the people. Rather than allowing the people to express their will through elections, a select group of persons determined who would be the leaders. This same caucus system introduced the petition style in which the ordinary people were made to march in a demonstration of solidarity and present a petition to the president for him to succeed himself, usually county after county presented petitions and these petitions took the place of elections, thus enabling Tubman to enjoy successive terms of office for twenty-seven unbroken years.

Tubman was also accused of nepotism by appointing family members to major positions of trust. Interestingly, everybody from Tubman's hometown called him "Cousin Shad." These were responses of the people to Tubman's method of patronage.

There is a need to revamp the political system to meet the demands of democracy. It may be necessary to elect local leaders, superintendents, and legislators so that they will seek the interest of the people who vote for them. When appointed by the president, there is a tendency to seek to please the president. The political system of Liberia needs to be strengthened and improved.

The legal/judicial system of any nation is the foundation of order. Liberia's legal system has been weighed in the balance and has been found wanting. The laws of Liberia need to be reviewed. Those that are unjust and unfair need to be repealed. Laws about land ownership, property, and inheritance should be reconsidered.

Cases that should be determined by a court of law were decided before reaching the court. Usually the president or a legislator interfered in the legal system. Many persons were above the law, thus rendering the law useless. The ordinary Liberian was cheated and did not benefit from the legal system, usually for lack of finances.

The writer has observed a rise in student deaths. Edward Gberi was strangled to death by a Lebanese merchant because he allegedly stole candy. The case went to the lower court, and the merechant was found guilty. An appeal to the Supreme Court led to demonstrations by students. Since then, the young people especially have viewed the system with mistrust and a good number have studied law. It is refreshing to note that the present National Bar Association has maintained some standards and is striving to introduce respect for the legal system.

The socieconomic system of Liberia has maintained a class struggle and is responsible for a high level of discontent. As a nation, revenues have not been equally distributed to the various sectors. Liberia exported raw materials and imported goods. The income of the average Liberian has not been commensurate with the inflation rate. The average income per month is five hundred Liberian dollars, which is roughly ten US dollars; no wonder corruption and other economic malpractice abound in Liberia.

When one looks all around, one can see foreigners, especially Lebanese and Indians, running the businesses and even teaching Liberians to do business. The government has not encouraged and prepared the people to take control of their own economy. Liberians need to be given priority in employment, and Liberian businesses need to be supported.

Certain percentages of taxes collected from the counties should be used toward the development of the county. There is a need for equitable distribution of wealth. Agriculture, which should be one of Liberia's strengths, is low. The problem can be attributed to the rubber and mining concessions, which hired laborers by providing food and other incentives. This is not to say the provision of incentives was a bad idea, but this should have been balanced by the government with the promotion of agriculture.

The problems that plagued Liberia internally are numerous. In this chapter, I have sought to point out some of these problems that may have contributed to the war. I contend that if Liberia is to return to normalcy and pursue a path of peace and development, we must address these problems.

SIX

BETTER LATE THAN NEVER

ATTEMPTS to find internal root causes of the civil war in Liberia was the focus of the previous chapter as we identified failed policies, systems, and institutions that resulted in the breakdown of social order. However, one cannot overlook the notion that there were also external factors that contributed to the decline of life in Liberia.

In no way can Liberia be justifiably described as not strategic enough to the United States of America. In an effort to accommodate the needs of the US during the two World Wars and in efforts to rebuild the West, Liberia made available its territory, though itself a sovereign nation, where a military air base was opened, a seaport was used by the US Navy, iron ore was extracted from the mines, rubber was planted and tapped. This writer seeks to get the point across that the war in Liberia could have been brought to an end if the US had played a more direct and constructive role. To downplay Liberia's importance is unfair to a nation that "bent over backward" for another nation it considers a traditional friend. America has a moral responsibility for helping end the Liberian war and restore it to normalcy.

A number of flash points in the history of Liberia, particularly during the course of the seven-year-old Liberian civil conflict, have recently generated heated discussions of US-Liberian relationships.

In mid-1990, the Liberian nation-state was on the verge of collapse. Numerous calls went out for international intervention to stabilize the situation. There was, in particular, a general expectation that the United States would intervene in what, for too long, many have viewed as an "unofficial American colony."

In June 1990, US warships with two thousand marines on board anchored off the Liberian coast with the official expressed instruction to evacuate US and other foreign nationals. The marines did not attempt to establish order, with then-President George Bush declaring that "Liberia is not worth (strategically) the life of a single marine."

Most Liberians, who are descendants of the American-Blacks and others brought up under the aegis of "Uncle Sam," would probably have accepted US intervention. But at a crucial point in August, 1990, something happened elsewhere in the world that diverted American attention and definitely ruled out any possibility of American intervention in Liberia: Iraq invaded Kuwait. This chapter argues that there exists a historical and cultural "traditional friendship" between Liberia and the United States. We will advance and support the view that the US has some moral obligation toward Liberia. Several opportunities were available to the US to stand up to these obligations during the Liberian crisis, but the US responses were not appropriate and timely. I believe that, although the response of the United States has been lukewarm in facilitating the end to the war in Liberia, it is better that concrete actions be taken now to urge Liberia on the road to democracy and progress.

Liberia was founded by various philanthropic organizations in the USA, the largest of which was the American Colonization Society (ACS). The ACS was formed mainly to assist free Blacks who were formerly slaves in America and had a desire to return to Africa. Those who were not free were promised freedom if they wanted to leave America.

Chattel slavery, as it was practiced in America, was a moral stigma on the history of that great Christian country. For more than 230 years Africans were forcibly uprooted from their homes and transported under inhumane conditions to North America where they slaved on plantations and provided labor to develop North America. Under these conditions, they became the property of their masters, nothing more.

The practice of slavery declined perhaps for many reasons, including the Industrial Revolution, which made the services of the slaves no longer necessary, and the awakening of the Christian conscience.

When the existence of slavery no longer propitious, America's options were many. America could have integrated the slaves, making them a part of its society. An effort apparently was made to purge American society of Blacks by relocating them within or near the US as a colony of Africans. The two attempts to locate the Africans in Louisana and in Texas failed because of the strong presence of Spanish and French cultures in those areas. Eventually, it was decided to take the Africans back to their continent of origin.

The combination of the desire of some Black people in America to return to Africa and the unwillingness of the American public to accommodate the "free people of color" in peaceful co-existence necessitated the formation of the American Colonization Society (ACS). Founded in the city of Philadelphia known as "the city of brotherly love," the organization was headed by Bushrod Washington, a relative of US President George Washington. The project was taken to Congress for approval and sponsorship. Although Congress gave $50,000 to support the project, the ACS did not become government-sponsored; it depended largely on individual philanthropists for its major source of support.

Through the ACS, the US government was provided an opportunity to establish a credible Black republic to its own credit and remove some of the shame of slavery from its history. But plans were not made to properly settle Liberia through organizing the commonwealth, providing educational facilities, setting up industries, and teaching the people the way of American-style democracy before a declaration of independence.

Due to this policy of noncolonialism on the part of America

toward Liberia, France and England encroached on and claimed a sizable portion of Liberia's territory with impunity. America missed an opportunity to prepare a great nation for a noble task of leading the whole of Africa toward independence.

The history of Liberia's founding is common knowledge. Although the ACS was the organization mainly responsible for the establishment of Liberia as a haven for Blacks everywhere, its agents were told "to exercise no power founded on the principle of colonization or other power than that of performing the benevolent offices," which were believed to be outlined in their manuals of instruction (*Liberia Bulletin*: 17).

The government of Liberia has always respected that position but only hoped that "the US would at all times and in every practicable way manifest a friendly interest in the colony planted so largely through its agency . . ." (*Liberia Bulletin*: 17). It seems as if America abhorred the opportunity to become too involved in Liberia's affairs and thus allowed the agents of the ACS and the settlers to run the affairs of the nation. At the same time, the US remained close enough to influence the destiny of Liberia and benefit therefrom. It is likely that the US, having been a colony of Great Britain, did not want to practice what it fought against, thus the name *American Colonization Society* was itself a misnomer. However, it is difficult to conclude concrete reasons underlying the avoidance attitude of America toward Liberia that kept the US from facilitating the development of a democratic nation-state.

During the years of Liberia's independence, the decline in interest by America became evident. In his inauguration address following his re-election, President Joseph Cheeseman attempted to provide an explanation for this absence of concern. He said that America accused Liberia of having "failed its mission" which was, it seemed, to form a state where all Blacks, regardless of origin, could find a home. Liberia was particularly criticized about its hinterland policy, which tended to exclude the indigenous population. America was against the idea of creating Liberia "as a slice of Georgia or South Carolina stuck on the West Coast of Africa" (*Liberia Bulletin*: 80). Liberia's hinterland policy, which had changed negatively from the early days of Liberia's first president, Joseph Jenkins Roberts, constantly came under sharp criticism; and it is believed to have been a contributing factor leading to the resignation of President William Coleman.

These problems should have encouraged a more practical and substantial involvement by America in guiding the affairs of Liberia. Being the "promoter and founder" of Liberia as a nation and having provided no training to the leaders in government or otherwise, except that which was gained through slavery, America had a moral responsibility for the success of Liberia.

One does not need to look far to realize that Liberia has passed the test of being a former American "colony" despite what the US attempts to communicate about its relationship to Liberia. In more ways than one, America's influence on Liberia and Liberia's status as an American "colony" was clear.

Early in Liberia's history, the United States dollar became legal tender in Liberia and, in fact, served as the official Liberian currency. It was in 1986 that President Samuel Doe replaced the US dollar with the Liberian dollar. The sentiment being expressed by some Liberians is the hope for the return to the US currency. The economic implications are not the concern of this writer at this point, but many Liberians declare the days of the US dollar as the "good old days."

Not only did the US currency form a part of the Liberian culture, the constitution of Liberia was based on the American constitution and was drafted by Simon Greenleaf, a Boston lawyer. This constitution served as the basis of governance in Liberia until the military coup d'etat in 1980 that overthrew the Tolbert government and suspended the constitution. The constitution remained suspended until it was revised in 1985; however, the essence of democracy as practiced in America remained enshrined in the revised constitution.

When one looks at the flag of the Republic of Liberia, one can see what is almost a carbon copy of the American flag, the exception being the number of stars and stripes. The makers of the flag, one can be certain, wanted to reflect their connection to the US as their pride at being "an American offspring."

The Capital of Liberia is named in honor and in memory of one-time American president, James Monroe. In order to show Liberia's love for America, the authorities changed the name of the Capital from "Christopolis" (City of Christ) to "Monrovia" (Monroe's way—US way).

The general Liberian culture as practiced alongside the traditional culture is American. The educational system, complete with its syllabus, textbooks, and teaching methods, the type of standard English spoken have American influence. The majority of Liberians who pursue graduate studies do so in the US, and since the 1980's, the number of Liberians attending American high schools and colleges has increased. The dress, even the foods to a large extent, though contributed by Liberia's indigenous tribes, have an American flavor added through fried chicken, collard greens, cabbage, and other foods. Religiously, Roman Catholic and Protestant denominations have found expression in Liberia.

The foregoing are obvious indications of Liberia's closeness to America because of historical and cultural ties. If America did not recognize Liberia as an unofficial colony, why was this great nation slow in recognizing Liberia's independence? Was it a fear that the slaves would finally earn a diplomatic place in Washington, DC? The political implications are many; but suffice it to say that Liberia viewed itself as a direct result of an American experiment and considered itself, if not a colony, a satellite offshoot of the United States.

Indeed, the whole world understands the friendship that exists between the United States and Liberia. America has had very little direct involvement in the development of Liberia and seems to have left the governance of the nation entirely up to its leadership. No industry, no university or college, no high school was built. The American Cooperative School, which operated in Monrovia prior to the war, was built for American Embassy staff children and the children of Americans and other internationals who wanted to attend. Those Liberians who could afford the exorbitant cost sent their children there.

If America wanted Liberia to become a Black nation where both settlers and natives would enjoy equality and if Liberia was not pursuing the fulfillment of that policy, means were available to America to pressure Liberia into living up to that expectation. How could the US feel justified in allowing people who had no experience in politics and government and whose only experience was the subservient life of the plantation to begin and successfully run a new nation? How did America expect the settlers to do it without guidance, knowing that this system required time and skill?

Liberia's problem is a reflection of America's policy of benign neglect. Though the government and people of Liberia are not totally without fault as was discussed in an earlier chapter, Liberia's attachment to America provided opportunities for America to assist this nation that struggled for true "Liberty," a byword of American democracy.

If America can earnestly search its conscience for a friend who has been true, Liberia will be mentioned because of the significant role Liberia has played in facilitating America's place as a superpower, an industrialized nation, and leader of the free world in its war efforts of 1939 to 1945.

America lost a first opportunity to make a difference in Liberia at the inception of the Liberian nation.

A second opportunity became available to the US to provide a basis for economic development in Liberia. After World War I the nations of Europe had expended much of their energies, and the center of power in the world was shifting. The United States and Japan were the two rising forces to be reckoned with.

Industrialization increased its pace; and America led the world in the production of coal, iron, steel, grain, and oil, among others. The production of cars also increased as America manufactured over half of the cars produced in the world. The need for rubber increased dramatically in the United States especially after the price of this commodity quadrupled in the world market.

Being an emerging superpower at the time, America did not want to be at the mercy of Britain and others who owned rubber plantations in Asia and Latin America. This made America go in search of a place to establish a rubber plantation. When it was discovered that Liberia was quite suitable for this venture, Liberia, out of love for this parent nation, gave one million acres of land upon which the Firestone Rubber Plantation was established through the signing of a ninety-nine-year lease in 1926.

The dynamics and chemistry of the relationship between the government of Liberia and Firestone is a topic of much debate. While it is true that the leadership of Liberia cannot escape some level of blame for the role Firestone played in the slow growth of the Liberian economy, the United States itself, the principal buyer and chief patron of Firestone, did not advocate a rubber industry or even a university or technical college for the people of Liberia.

By failing to assist Liberia in strengthening its economy, America was accused of exploitation and possible suppression. Knowing how accessible Liberia is to American influence and presence, the great nation took advantage of the smaller one. More importantly, America lost an opportunity to take credit for the building of a vibrant economy.

If "opportunity knocks but once," as it is usually said, this was disproved when another avenue for facilitating a sustainable economy was presented to America for Liberia. The peace that followed World War I was not firm. The rise of dictators in Europe and the failure of the League of Nations to become inclusive and influential enough soon posed another threat to the world. This threat became a reality in 1939 with the outbreak of World War II. The US did not become directly involved in the war until 1941. The war was fought in most parts of Europe, parts of North Africa, and parts of Asia.

This battle in North Africa was mainly for control of the Suez Canal, which provided direct access from the West to the East, or from Southern Europe through to the "oil rich Middle East" on to Asia. While most of the Allied and Axis nations had colonies in Africa that aided them in maintaining the war, the great United States had none. There was a need for a country that would provide land in a strategically located area for the construction of an airport where American planes would stop and refuel to and from North Africa and Southern Europe. Liberia was that strategically located country that made land available on which an air force military base was constructed. Later a waterway was given by Liberia to America to build a naval base. While the naval base was under construction, the war ended and America's need for Liberia ended. Thus the project was never completed.

Despite Liberia's contribution to America's development and the role Liberia played in buttressing America's success in the war, the air base constructed was never turned into an international airport. It was not until the 1970's that President Tolbert prepared the airport to become the Roberts International Airfield. The seaport remained underdeveloped and was used as a freeport.

Even during the Cold War, Liberia was used as a communication center for all US diplomatic and security operations. Liberia remained strategic because many of the nations in Africa had colonial loyalty that the US could not penetrate easily, but Liberia kept its loyalty to the United States. By being in Liberia, America was able to establish its presence in Africa.

When the Cold War ended and the Soviet Union collapsed, the US seemed to have no more interest in or use for Liberia. America withdrew much of its vital equipment while other equipment was turned over to the government of Liberia. Liberia, it must be noted, did not make America pay for the use of its sovereign territory as other nations in Europe and Asia did.

So America lost a second opportunity to make Liberia a democratic nation to its credit. By helping Liberia, as America ought to have done, it is safe to say that probably the civil rights movement in the US would not have been so tension-filled.

A third opportunity knocked on America's door to make America what it was meant to be from the beginning. In 1989, the civil war in Liberia began. By early 1990, Cable News Network (CNN) and other major news media in America came to Liberia to expose the war and possibly encourage America to intervene and bring this nightmare to an end before it got out of hand.

But as soon as the Gulf War broke out, all the news media packed their things and left Liberia. The only news coming out of Liberia was from the British Broadcasting Corporation (BBC) through the sacrificial efforts of its correspondent, Elizabeth Blunt.

In May of 1990, a peace demonstration of about fifty thousand people led by the author presented a statement to the US Ambassador accredited near Monrovia at the time. In that statement, we asked the US to intervene so that Liberians may not destroy themselves and their country. The ambassador told the peace demonstrators that the civil war was an internal matter and that we, Liberians, should go and solve it ourselves.

The US has lost three major opportunities to let the world know that it could make a difference in Liberia and that it is truly a nation of democracy that seeks to strengthen those nations that aspire for the noble goals of freedom and justice as Liberia has.

Let me hasten to add that when anarchy finally descended on the nation and a humanitarian disaster was pending, it was the United States that helped Liberia with food and medicine to the tune of four hundred million dollars. As ECOMOG, the military arm of ECOWAS, tried to create some semblance of law and order, America facilitated its operations through the provision of logistics, moral support, and in other ways probably not known to the nonmilitary observer. America has been a recent advocate of peace in Liberia and is becoming more and more active in Liberia's struggle toward peace.

Can this be enough? When the nation of Israel was established, America helped it become a nation. Today, we understand that billions and billions of dollars of US aid goes to Israel each year. Israel and Liberia have much in common. Those who founded both Liberia and Israel migrated mainly from America. Both groups have suffered shamefully through the holocaust and through slavery. We believe America has the means and the will to help Liberia rise from the ashes of destruction.

At the end of World War II, the Marshall Plan proposed by the then-US Secretary of State, George C. Marshall, asked

America to support and assist European countries that had been at war. This developmental assistance was "not against any country or doctrine but against hunger, poverty, desperation and chaos." Liberia needs a Marshall Plan because of the threat of hunger, poverty, desperation, disease, and chaos that looms over our nation.

No matter what America thinks and/or feels about Liberia, Liberia is its "offspring" or creation. Maybe in the strict sense of the word, Liberia may not have been a "colony" of America, but all indications point to Liberia as a nation founded through the instrumentality of America and needing America's support for its existence. Public sentiment or public policy may have been responsible for America's response to Liberia, but this does not excuse America from its moral obligation to equip, prepare, and facilitate Liberia's democratic, economic, and social growth—even helping Liberia avoid this civil war.

As we enter the third phase of Liberia's history, the opportunities present themselves to the United States to empower Liberia to become a great nation. Now is the time because, as the Americans like to put it, "better late than never."

SEVEN

NEIGHBORS INDEED

COMMON saying in Liberia goes like this: "I was born in Liberia, I will live in Liberia, I will die in Liberia." This statement not only reinforces the love Liberians have for their country but it also emphasizes that Liberians are at a disadvantage when they have, over the years, refused to travel to other African countries and accept other Africans as their brothers and sisters. Until the inception of the civil war in December 1989, going to any African country for any reasons, other than as an ambassador or attending international conferences, was not only unacceptable, but discouraged. In their attempt to save their lives during the war, Liberians sought refuge in neighboring African nations. How did they fare? How were they accepted? These are the questions addressed in this chapter.

Indeed, "being away" for most Liberians, even for those living in remote villages, often meant going to America or going to Europe. This attitude and behavior prevented many Liberians from traveling to other African countries until we were forced to flee there by the hundreds and thousands when the war escalated.

Of course, out of necessity, we employed other Africans in government ministries and other service industries to the extent that some African brothers and sisters acquired better skills than some Liberians. They were employed at the expense of many Liberians. However, they were never welcome, accepted, or treated as fellow Africans.

One would expect, and logically so, that given such a background, Liberians would hesitate to enter other West African countries whenever there was a problem in Liberia. On the contrary, we Liberians fled for our lives when we felt that Liberia had no more room for our existence and future. To the surprise and relief of most Liberians, the West African countries, particularly the Ivory Coast and Guinea, opened their doors wide and accepted us without any hindrance. Some did so, realizing that this could bring social and economic hardship on their people.

But as we moved into their countries in large numbers, it became apparent that the host countries were not socially, economically, or emotionally prepared to accept countless numbers of people. Thus, not only the influx of people was restricted, but each country instituted different programs for the newly arrived Liberians.

In the Ivory Coast, particularly in the towns along the borders, Liberians were considered guests and tourists. Thus, even though we were officially refugees, we never lived in refugee camps because there were none. We were expected to live in any community, and the freedom to live anywhere helped us move freely and establish small businesses that made our living easier. In fact, many Ivorians, especially the common people, did everything they could to welcome and accommodate the Liberian refugees.

Churches were allowed to operate freely throughout the Ivory Coast. As a result, Liberians established Christian churches in Danane, Tabou, Man, and other towns where Liberians live.

Ghana was one of the most hospitable nations when it came to Liberian refugees. Originally, Liberians found a "home away from home" in Ghana. According to the earliest refugees, when the first ship arrived in Ghana, their reception was warm and friendly. Food, medicines, and shelter were made available.

The story changed when Liberians began to show ingratitude to the Ghanaians by making a fuss of the food and accent of their hosts. Coupled with the length of the war, Liberians seemed to have worn out their welcome.

As time went on, and because of the influx of Liberians, refugees were no longer allowed into Ghana. Even so, the security people and most common Ghanaians still welcome Liberian refugees. An example of this attitude of many Ghanaians is when I was traveling to Ghana in August 1996. We got to the border and the security refused us entry. After much discussion, the security chief told me that the Ghanaian government had ordered that no Liberian should be allowed to enter Ghana. After I pleaded with him, he allowed us to pass. Other stories tell of many common Ghanians assisting Liberian refugees to enter Ghana as their relatives.

Not only Guinea, Ghana, and the Ivory Coast accepted Liberian refugees; other West African countries such as Sierra Leone, Benin, Nigeria, and others followed suit and accepted Liberian refugees. During this civil war in Liberia, Liberians have traveled all over the globe. A friend of mine told me the other day that there are Liberians residing in New Zealand.

The warm and friendly reception that we Liberians received from our brothers and sisters does not negate the harsh and sometimes cruel treatment that has been meted against us by a few, but influential, individuals in the host countries. In the Ivory Coast, security personnel, particularly the ones on the highways, and the city police were noted for harassing, intimidating, and beating innocent Liberian refugees for no reason other than the fact that they were Liberians.

To be sure, Liberians of all walks of life have countless stories to tell in this regard. But one personal experience worth mentioning is this. One day, we were traveling from Abidjan Airport to Abobo by way of the zoo. Suddenly we were stopped by a group of police. I showed them my diplomatic passport with my picture in episcopal clerical clothing; but it made no difference to them. They searched our luggage and our handbags, turning everything upside down. When I protested that as an elderly man and a bishop of the United Methodist Church in Liberia they should not subject me to such a humiliating search especially since I carried a diplomatic passport, the commander of the police told me, "If you do not like what we did to you, go home!" If such an incident occurred to me, what may have happened to countless other Liberians?

Even so, the Ivory Coast and Ghana rank at the top of the line when it comes to the treatment and reception of refugees in West Africa. The type of reception described above was probably due to "reception fatigue" or "host fatigue" that resulted from the length of the war. As stated earlier there were times when the security forces of both Ghana and the Ivory Coast were generous, understanding, and considerate. No doubt there were times when they exercised the refugee policy liberally.

Unlike in the Ivory Coast where Liberian refugees were at liberty to move freely, in Guinea, Liberian refugees were restricted to live either in the frontier towns and villages or in refugee camps. Anyone found out of bounds was arrested, beaten, and even killed without due process of law. A few Liberians may have lived in the capital city, Conakry; this was an exception, not the norm. In many parts of Guinea where Liberians had to reside, the refugees were not allowed to fetch firewood or cut sticks from the forest, unless there was an agreement for some compensation to be given the owner of the forest. Life in Guinea for the Liberian refugees was not "a piece of cake," for they experienced extreme hardships. This was surprising because Guineans who lived and worked in Liberia prior to the war lived and worked without much hindrance.

Between 1989 and 1990, the Republic of Sierra Leone opened its doors and welcomed hundreds, if not thousands, of refugees. But as time went on, most likely due to a combination of factors, Liberians in Sierra Leone became unwelcome to the point where, in order to travel from Monrovia to Freetown, one needed an official letter from the Sierra Leonian Embassy in Monrovia.

In traveling from Kennedy International Airport in New York to Monrovia, one of the likely carriers is KLM, the Dutch airlines. KLM flies into Freetown where one has to take a connecting flight to Monrovia on a local carrier known as the

Weasua Air Transport (WAT). In New York, if a Liberian is traveling on KLM to Monrovia via Freetown, boarding is denied until clearance is received from Freetown. This is due to a Sierra Leonian government policy of strict transit regulations for Liberians.

Though Liberians have received mixed treatment in West Africa, West Africans who lived and worked in Liberia have enjoyed Liberian hospitality. Many Liberians were denied jobs and other privileges that were given to foreigners, especially West Africans.

The war has taught many lessons to Liberians, but one message that has taken root in the hearts and lives of Liberians is the love of the land and the appreciation of one another. Liberians are ready to move their country forward. It is a must.

EIGHT

THANK GOD FOR ECOMOG

AUGUST 24 remains fresh in the hearts and minds of all Liberians. This day is set aside to celebrate the unfurling of the national ensign; it is also the day on which the first contingent of ECOMOG soldiers arrived in Monrovia to help restore sanity to Liberia. Their reception in Monrovia was mixed. Some hailed their arrival as peace brokers and saw them as deserving both our cooperation and support. Others, especially those in areas known as "Greater Liberia," regarded ECOMOG soldiers as a hindrance to their desire and quest to capture and rule Liberia by military might. Therefore, they made a concerted effort to discredit, and if possible, destroy the initiatives of the West African sub-region.

In fact, on many occasions, ECOWAS was portrayed as those meddling in the internal affairs of Liberia at the expense of its sovereignty. They were accused of derailing the peace process in Liberia by sending foreign troops against the wishes of the Liberian people.

To make matters worse, from the onset of ECOMOG's arrival until recently they were not authorized by the leaders of ECOWAS to exercise full military power in subduing the warring factions and getting them to accept disarmament. Furthermore, the chairman of ECOWAS did not exercise enough diplomatic and political clout in order to speed up or to expedite the task of ECOMOG in bringing peace to Liberia.

Also, while European nations were expecting the United States government to initiate the mobilization of the international community to respond to Liberia by helping ECOMOG, America, at the time, did not see the need or urgency to do so. Rather, the US declared on many occasions that what was happening in Liberia was an internal problem, left to be solved by Liberians.

Another added factor that made ECOMOG's task more difficult is the relationship between French-speaking and English-speaking members of ECOWAS. Neither wanted the other to succeed in bringing peace to Liberia because it would mean credit for one group. Hence, even though the commanding generals of ECOMOG came from Ghana and Nigeria, substantial progress in the peace process was slow. This may explain why ECOWAS, with all its military and economic power, was unable to bring the situation in Liberia under control speedily.

A third element that served as an obstacle to ECOMOG's task of bringing peace to Liberia was the lack of goodwill on the part of the international community. The European Union (EU) and the US have not been as helpful militarily. Promises made by the US and by nations of the EU were not as forthcoming, yet ECOMOG still struggled to resolve the problem in Liberia. Given these difficulties and knowing what ECOMOG has endured in order to bring peace in Liberia, Liberians have nothing to give ECOMOG but praise and gratitude for their achievement.

The first thing ECOMOG noticed when they arrived in Monrovia was the deplorable condition of the people of Monrovia. Liberians were dying by the thousands from hunger and diseases. Thus, the first needs ECOMOG forces saw and attended to were the humanitarian ones. They began to share their meager resources and rations with the dying population they met. ECOMOG soldiers were seen feeding children, the elderly, and mothers with babies. The nurses and doctors in the first contingent worked around the clock to save lives. This, in my considered opinion, is one of the major reasons why the people in Monrovia considered ECOMOG troops as their friends.

Having achieved their primary objective, which was to save lives of the starving Liberians, ECOMOG forces began creating a breathing space for those in Monrovia to live and work. Thus, they commenced pushing the NPFL rebels and all those whom they felt were hindrances to the peace process. In the process of this engagement, the terrain being unknown to the ECOMOG soldiers, hundreds of them were killed and many were wounded. Not only that, but citizens from ECOMOG-contributing countries who were journalists were arrested and killed simply because they were from ECOMOG countries.

The second field commander of ECOMOG was General Joshua Dogoyaro of Nigeria. With his military skills and experience, he wanted to end the war in Liberia within six months. This meant using all the military equipment at his disposal. But because Liberians felt we needed to solve our problems through dialogue, General Dogoyaro's plans were never realized. Had we listened to him and allowed him to do his job, other warring factions would not have emerged, there would not have been "Operation Octopus," nor a "Fall of Gbarnga"; and surely there would not have been an "April 6th war."

In other words, if the good general had been able to follow his plan for bringing the war to an end, untold sufferings of Liberians, destruction of lives and properties, displacement of thousands of Liberians internally and externally, and the near destruction of the future of Liberia would not have happened.

With the departure of General Dogoyaro, one would expect that ECOMOG would have been discouraged and left Liberia. But no, ECOWAS nations continued to send their soldiers and share their meager resources with Liberia. As ECOMOG soldiers came, they moved into the interior of Liberia at the expense of their lives. Many died, including those who were killed in Vahun, those who were abducted in Gbarnga during the "Fall of Gbarnga," and those killed on the Bomi highway and other places.

To date, General S. Victor Malu, General Oloritu, and other outstanding generals and soldiers of ECOMOG have a special place in the hearts of Liberians. This is why it is common to hear Liberians, even those in the interior of the country say, "Thank God for ECOMOG."

NINE

LIBERIA WILL RISE AGAIN

THE situation in Liberia is not totally hopeless. Liberia will rise again, not to where it was, but beyond where it was.

In Liberia a common saying, "In times of peace, prepare for war," is being turned around: "In times of war, prepare for peace."

The war in Liberia has now ended. Peace prevails in the country. Now we must begin addressing Liberia's peacetime needs. The government cannot be expected to tread this path single-handedly. Community-based NGO's, individuals, community and civic groups should join forces and support the movement toward a better Liberia. Several elements that should be addressed in order to help Liberia arrive at a desired state will be the emphasis of this closing chapter.

The war in Liberia has introduced a culture of violence into our society. Young people are accepting the notion that they can obtain power through one means—the use of force. Our society has become saturated with arms; the use of threats and intimidation to achieve what one wants has become commonplace. Young people need special attention to help expand their views of achieving power.

Worst of all, education has been downplayed as a priority. This tendency goes back to the years of the revolution when Doe was compared to Moses, who was described as having ascended to a leadership position without formal education.

The church sought to correct the idea that Moses received no formal education, that being in the palace of the pharoah exposed him to the best thinkers available, and that Moses *was* an educated man. Attempts were also made to refute the concept that education was not important; and eventually, President Doe himself enrolled in the University of Liberia, earned one degree, and was planning to pursue another before the war disrupted his plans.

Somehow, this war has produced some "noveau riche" who want to institutionalize the "wealth without education" idea. This concept is detrimental to the good of any society, and the Liberian people cannot afford to build their country on this view. The need for education and skill training cannot be overlooked. It may be to the advantage of the nation if skill training or vocational education is introduced as early as junior high school. This way, if persons want to continue with vocational education they can pursue advanced training; and if they are interested in academic education, they will have avocations that could be used to their benefit. In any case, the value of education must be upheld to undermine the view that one does not need to be educated to live a fulfilled, rich, and satisfying life.

The war has also brought a lack of respect for our humanity, for human rights, and for the elderly. The intense and open brutality shown by combatants has affected Liberia adversely. After seeing how people were tortured and killed, after seeing corpses lying around, and after blaming the older people for the national problems, attitudes toward one another are negative. Human rights mean nothing. Many Liberians have concluded that they cannot expect justice or fair redress of their complaints when their rights are violated. The aged feel isolated and dehumanized because of neglect. If the leaders and the common people insist on order in the society, and human rights are promoted, this problem can be solved. We must promote civic education in the schools and for the public, so that the citizens will understand that they have a duty to themselves and to one another and that they have a responsibility to uphold the government, especially in promoting positive principles.

Liberians believed that this country could be properly run by an iron-handed leader whose Draconian style will set things right. For almost twenty years, Liberians have seen the iron-handed leadership of Doe, Taylor, and the leaders of the warring factions. Without reservation one can conclude that Liberians should no longer hold that view. Liberians need a tough but flexible leader, one with compassion, a sound head, and a considerate heart who understands and touches the people. Liberia needs a leader who will provide employment, support better education, produce a sound health system, encourage participation by the people, and seek the common good of all.

The war has also brought deeper division and deep-rooted antagonism along ethnic lines. The Krahns, from which Doe hailed, still feel they are the target of national ridicule and disgrace. The April 6 catastrophe did nothing to reduce this feeling. As a result the Krahns are on the defensive, and many of them are still bent on avenging the death of Doe. Others believe the Krahns must rule Liberia in order to be vindicated.

The Manos and Gios feel justified in their revenge of the brutal slaying of their hero, Thomas Quiwonkpa, and the many atrocities leveled against them by the Doe regime. Many of them are insecure and do not trust the Krahns. They believe, at least many do, that the Manos and Gios should be in power to keep themselves from being marginalized.

The Mandingoes, who have always been at a disadvantageous position, are now attempting to carve a place for themselves in national life. Whether the deep-rooted resentment of Mandingoes for their social and business practices, which some believe were discriminatory in nature, still exists is hard to say. While they are clamoring for recognition as bona fide Liberians, the danger exists that some may take their case to the extreme.

The Congos, who have always been among the elite, have been the subject of ridicule for some time now. A good number see themselves as divinely selected to lead Liberia. Though the NPFL argued it attacked the Doe government because of corruption and economic crimes, some quarters argue that Taylor, himself of the Congo stock, is seeking to reinstitute the Congo rule into Liberia. Doe was the common enemy that attracted the Manos/Gios and Taylor to each other. It is easy to see how the anger of the Manos/Gios against what Doe did to them was exploited by Taylor. This may explain the defection from the NPFL by men like Dokie, Supuwood, and Woewiyu, who suspect that when all is said and done they will have been instrumental in getting the Congo people back into the executive mansion.

The Congos themselves have to forgo the revenge of the "thirteen" who were publicly executed in 1980. Unless they do, one can predict a vicious cycle of revenge and hatred spiraling the nation into more anarchy.

We need a national policy that will unite all Liberian people. We need a collective ideology that is cohesive in nature. When one considers the history of Liberia, one will realize that all Liberians are settlers. One group settled from the Sudanic region in the heart of Africa. The factors that led to their migration to this part of West Africa included possibly the movement of Islam from the north, epidemics, famine, and even adventure. The other group settled here from North America where they had been slaves. It is fair to conclude that "the love of liberty" brought all Liberians to this land that is owned by every Liberian. No Liberian is more Liberian than another.

If a nation is a group of people united by some commonalities such as ancestry, language, customs, and traditions, we need to find and stress those commonalities that unite and link us together. The war has driven a wedge of division among us and we must overcome it. We must not only become true nationalists but also patriots who put Liberian interests first.

Presently, there is a scramble for areas containing gold, diamonds, and other natural resources. Liberia is our country. Those mining these resources and selling them are stealing from themselves. They are delaying the peace process because they believe they will lose these opportunities. This does not have to be the case. These persons could establish mining cooperatives, register as a legitimate entity, and continue mining or logging legally, paying revenue to the government that would in turn use these taxes to develop the nation.

As we move toward a better Liberia, we must learn the lessons of being in exile. Liberians tend to be hospitable to strangers; yet they can be boastful, arrogant, eponymous, argumentative, and boisterous. Stories of Liberians in exile in West Africa reveal the need to change these attitudes. When the refugees first arrived in these host countries, the nationals received the refugees with open hearts and arms. The unappreciative tendency of the refugees, coupled with the lingering of the war, made them wear out their welcome.

Liberians in exile need to realize that they can make the best of a bad situation. They should be preparing to contribute to the building of a vibrant society and make it functional. They should take advantage of training opportunities and acquire needed skills. The negative impression from money doubling, commonly known as "Black Money" or "B.M.," and prostitution do not help the image of Liberians in those countries.

The prophecy of Zechariah to the Jewish exiles can be applied to Liberia:

> In the whole land, says the LORD,
> two-thirds shall be cut off and perish,
> and one-third shall be left alive.
> And I will put this third into the fire
> and refine them as one refines silver,
> and test them as gold is tested.
> They will call on my name,
> and I will answer them.
> I will say, "They are my people";
> and they will say, "The LORD is our God."
> Zechariah 13:8-9

All Liberians need to put their minds on one thing and pray for it—that one thing is peace. As long as we pray factional prayers, we will be divided; and even when God brings peace we will not appreciate it.

Being in exile should teach Liberians the importance of sticking together. They should love and support one another. They should also appreciate being in a wider context, the West

African region. For many years, many Liberians did not travel beyond their own borders. If they did, it was the United States that was considered a second home. After the war, Liberians must continue to nourish the relationships established with other Africans. Liberian culture will be richer as a result.

Finally, as we look forward to the rise of Liberia, our faith in God must remain undaunted. I once met a United Methodist lady of substance in the Ivorian border town of Danane who had lost everything she had. I tried to console her but she replied joyfully, "I thank God for everything, Bishop, because though I did not bring anything with me to Danane, at least I brought my body and my Jesus." This is the kind of undiminished faith Liberians need to hold. The friendship Liberians enjoy with Jesus is not wartime friendship but a relationship spanning many years. Their faith in God has kept many Liberians, though destitute, striving to make it.

Let me hasten to say that some Liberians have turned to the dark side and have come to depend on the amulets and fetishes of witchcraft and voodoo, but those Liberians who are faithful to Jesus are making an impact.

As traumatic and stressful as the war has been, Liberians who are rooted in the Christian faith can say with the apostle Paul,

> We are afflicted in every way, but not crushed; perplexed, but not driven to despair; persecuted, but not forsaken; struck down, but not destroyed.
> 2 Corinthians 4:8-9

Our faith in God is the source of our strength, our comfort, and our hope. Liberia will one day rise from gloom to glory, from darkness to marvelous light, from despair to hope. Liberia will rise again from a people scattered to a people gathered in strength and unity, from being lost to being found. Liberia shall rise from the mire to the solid rock, from the quicksand of destruction to the heights of development. I am convinced, I am positive that Liberia shall rise again.

Liberians must be optimistic about themselves and about

their nation. We need to look on the positive side and be determined to put this phantasmagora behind us. We must work to bring into existence a nation where there will be love, respect, acceptance, and tolerance of one another. People will differ; but difference should not cause enmity, and opposition does not have to mean antagonism.

In order to weave the fabric of our society together, we need to cultivate the moral values necessary to maintain standards of dignity. Family values must be upheld. Living together without being married should be discouraged. Efforts should be made to eliminate having children out of wedlock. Divorce should not be a factor of consideration in marital problems. The age of consent should be raised from sixteen to twenty-one.

The church must continue to be the watcher and shepherd of the nation. The church, though not agreed on the level of involvement in political and social affairs, must realize that it has a responsibility to the state. Paul is right that "there is no authority except from God, and those authorities that exist have been instituted by God" (Romans 13:1). The church must see to it the government carries out God's will for God's people.

Christianity must continue to make its presence felt in Liberia. It must continue the holistic approach to ministry to meet the total needs of the person. Some Christians may have failed Liberia, but Christianity has never failed Liberia. The principles and tenents of the faith are still valid. Members may need to be disciplined a little more rather than leaving it up to the individual. The church must guide, direct, encourage, and edify its members so that they live exemplary lives.

Liberia will rise again. The war has ended. The causes were many. Those who benefited were also many. The factors that prolonged the war were not only external; they were internal as well. Yet, despite the odds, we believe Liberia will come from the grave and live as a new nation.

God is with us, but we must become involved in determining our destiny. A great Liberian political activist once said, "We must pray as if it all depends on God and work as if it all depends on us."

When Liberia rises, her star will shine brighter than it did before; and "nations shall come to [God's] light and kings to the brightness of [God's] dawn" to quote Isaiah 60:3. This hope in God and faith in ourselves will lead us to a land flowing with milk and honey. For inasmuch as Christ, our Lord and Savior, was arrested, ridiculed, crucified, dead, and buried but rose from the grave, we too will surely rise again!